VW Transporter and Microbus
Specification Guide 1967–1979

Vincent Molenaar and Alexander Prinz

The Crowood Press

First published in 2005 by
The Crowood Press Ltd
Ramsbury, Marlborough
Wiltshire SN8 2HR

www.crowood.com

British Library Cataloguing-in-Publication Data
A catalogue record for this book is available from the British Library.

ISBN 1 86126 765 7

Whilst every effort has been made to ensure the accuracy of all material, the authors and
publisher cannot accept liability for loss resulting from error, misstatement, inaccuracy or
omission contained herein. The authors welcome any correction or additional information.

Typeset and designed by D & N Publishing
Hungerford, Berkshire.

Printed and bound in Singapore by Craft Print International.

contents

preface

As a child I felt a great affinity with vehicles of all types, especially older ones. Finally, in 1999, I decided it was time to buy one for myself. I knew very little about them, but when I saw an old VW Bus for sale in a small town in Süd-Westfalen in Germany, I fell for its colour and its unique shape. I looked at the cutaway illustration of the T2a from the operating manual, which was displayed on the windscreen, and decided to take a test drive. It was very rusty, but the engine still ran well. It was a '69 T2a Microbus with double sliding doors painted in Savanna Beige, and on a whim I decided to buy it. With this, the flames of my passion were inflamed.

I spent many hours restoring the Microbus, before moving on to my next project, in 2001 – a '70 T2a Panelvan in relatively good condition, to which I returned the look of the first owner, 'Klaus Esser KG'. The vehicle identification certificate of this Bus, which I got from the Volkswagen AutoMuseum, had some M- and Group- codes on it that even the specialists could not crack. There was no information available on the internet or in the VW Bus literature about the codes, except some basic information on the web page of the Dutch T2 enthusiast Vincent Molenaar. After doing some research on those mysterious codes in the VW archives and compiling some fascinating information about the Bay Window Bus, I felt that I had to put it all together in a comprehensive guide.

I would like to acknowledge the assistance of Lothar Brune (thanks for your support), Rainer Esser, Hansjörg Fricke (HF), Alexander Gromow (AG) (thanks for your efforts), Harald Hohnholz (HH), Uwe Mergelsberg (UM), Kees Mieremet (KM), Karl Nachbar (KN), Christine Neefe, Aribert Kolms, Andreas Plogmaker (APS) (thanks for the great 'last-minute' pictures), Roland Röttges (RR), Volker Seitz, Axel Steiner, Michael Steinke (MS) (special thanks for proofreading the text), Wilhelm Thiele (WT), Eric Trinczek (ET), Olaf Weddern, Susanne Wiersch, Eckbert von Witzleben and Joachim Wölfer (JW). A number of companies/relief organizations provided amazing pictures: Arbeiter Samariter Bund (ASB), Avacon GmbH (A), Bahlsen GmbH & Co. KG (B), Bischoff & Hamel Zweigniederlassung der Automobil Vertriebsgesellschaft mbH (BH), Edeka Verlag GmbH (E), ExxonMobil Central Europe Holding GmbH (EM), Alfred Kärcher GmbH & Co. KG (AK), Kraft Foods Deutschland GmbH (K), Landespolizeidirektion Schleswig-Holstein (PSH), Malteser Hilfsdienst e.V. (MHD), Miele & Cie. GmbH & Co. (M), Niedersächsische Wach- und Schließgesellschaft Eggeling & Schorling KG (NW), Otto Versand GmbH & Co. KG, Polizei Braunschweig (PB), Polizeipräsidium München (PM), Pon's Automobielhandel B.V. (P), Seba Dynatronic (SD), Archiv Björn Steiger Stiftung (BS), Stiftung AutoMuseum Volkswagen (SAV), Stiftung Rheinisch-Westfälisches Archiv zu Köln (R) and Vaillant GmbH (V). Volkswagen Nutzfahrzeuge helped in locating specific photographs and information about the T2. Pictures without proof of origin are from the author's personal archive or were issued by the press department of Volkswagen Light Commercial Vehicles.

Thanks to Friederike for her patience and support.

Alexander Prinz, Braunschweig (Germany), November 2004

In the early 1990s I was an avid collector of Coca-Cola cans and I soon found that I needed a big car in order to visit swap meets around the country – empty cans take a lot of space. At about the same time, I was studying with Volkswagen-freak Jens Zeemans, who talked me out of buying a Trabant Stationwagen and into the purchase of a 1978 VW Kombi. Soon the Kombi replaced the hobby for which it had been bought in the first place. In October 1996 I bought a 1976 Bay Window Crew cab as a donor for the Kombi. While parting the car out, I stumbled across a small metal tag. Jens Zeemans told me it probably had something to do with optional extras, or 'M-codes'. I could find little information about it on the internet, just a small list on the M-plate in the Split Window Bus. I joined the *Type2.com* mailing list and asked if anyone could help. Ron van Ness (USA) replied to my request and sent a list of M-codes he found on a microfiche – he even typed it all into the computer from the fiche reader screen!

Ron van Ness's list was the beginning of my investigation. In 1997 I started an internet page about the Bay Window M-plate and its codes, which was soon moved to the server of *Type2.com*. It was at about this time that I got in touch with Erik Meltzer and Andreas Plogmaker (both from Germany). Erik supplied me with more M-codes and with Andreas I exchanged M-plate codes. Around the year 2000 Alexander Prinz contacted me in relation to my M-code site. He was able to gain even more M-code info via his job at Volkswagen.

Since I started the M-code web page in 1997, I have received lots of feedback and questions from Bay Window owners who want to know more about their Bus. Many people supplied me with additional info on their Bus, which gave me a good basis for research. It has given the data written in this book an extra dimension of reliability; not only did we look at what the original VW documentation told us, but we also related it to the Buses that are out there. As a result, detailed info could be added on model years, export markets and so on. After a few years of email-correspondence, Alexander came up with the idea of writing a book together. At almost the same time David Eccles contacted me to ask if I was interested in doing the sequel of his *VW Transporter and Microbus: Specification Guide 1950–1967*.

Many thanks go to: the people of *Type2.com* for kindly hosting my M-plate pages; all the Bay Window owners who sent me the M-plates of their Buses and those whom I bothered at meetings with my M-plate questions; and the members of the *Type2.com* mailing list for answering many of my questions during the years.

Also many thanks go to the three major M-plate providers over the years: Willy Seegers, Sjef van Ginneken and Peter Witkamp. Furthermore, I would like to thank Jens Zeemans, David Eccles, Robert Markus of the Politiemuseum Apeldoorn, Klaas Niemeijer (KLN), Tom van Wissen (TvW), Gjalt Erkelens (GE), Peter and Mary Royall, and Pon's Automobielhandel B.V.

Should you have any remarks about this book, or questions relating to it, please feel free to contact us via e-mail at: info@t2-specification-guide.com.

Vincent Molenaar, Amsterdam (The Netherlands), November 2004

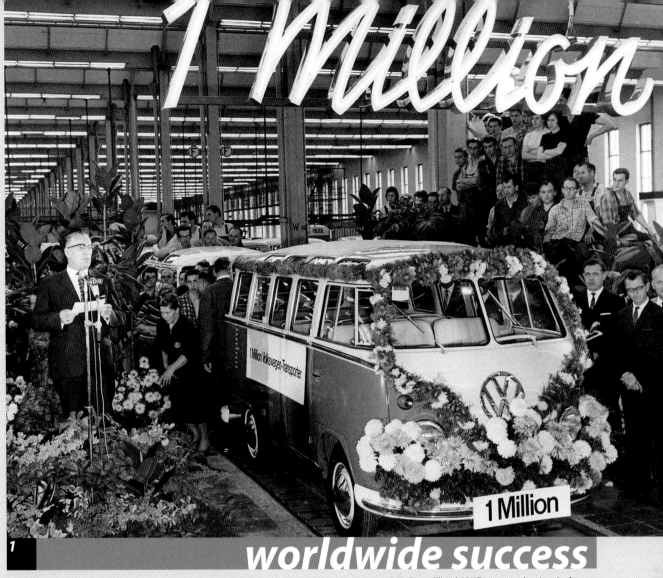

1

worldwide success

1962: One millionth VW Transporter leaving the factory.

A NEW IDEA AND A NEW FACTORY

Pon's Inspiration

It was the Dutch Volkswagen importer Ben Pon who laid the foundation for the success story of the VW Transporter. In 1947, two years after the end of the Second World War, Pon tried to get a licence from the British military authority to export cars from the British-occupied zone of Germany to the Netherlands. The head of this authority happened to be Major Hirst, then manager of the Volkswagenwerk. The only model produced by the company in Wolfsburg at this time was the VW Beetle. After meeting Major Hirst at his residence at the British military authority in Minden (Westfalen), Pon went to visit the Volkswagenwerk in Wolfsburg. He made an important discovery there: the so-called 'Plattenwagen', developed in 1946 for transportation purposes on the company's premises. These motorized trolleys were based on a Beetle chassis, with an extended loading area and a simple open cabin for the driver in the back, positioned over its engine.

Ben Pon was intrigued by the simple concept, and immediately saw that there might be a need for such a transportation vehicle in the Netherlands. However, the Dutch Road Authorities would not allow him to import it as it was; an open, unprotected cabin cab at the back

VW Plattenwagen.

5

of the vehicle seemed to be rather dangerous in a vehicle destined for regular traffic conditions.

However, Pon was not prepared to give up easily on his idea. On 23 April 1947, he sketched in his notebook a simple outline for a commercial transport vehicle with a van body. It had a driver's seat positioned in the front, the engine over the rear axle and an approximate distance between front and rear tyres of 2m. The gross weight was, assuming a similar weight distribution, 750kg per axle.

In January 1948 the Volkswagenwerk was handed over to the newly founded Federal Republic of Germany, under new general director Heinz Heinrich Nordhoff, a former engineer of Opel (General Motors). Ben Pon arranged a meeting with Nordhoff and showed him his ideas for the construction of a VW Transporter, which would be the second variant on the Beetle. Intrigued by the idea, Nordhoff instructed his head designer,

engineer Dr Alfred Haesner, to start immediately on the new project. The project was given the number EA 7 ('EA' representing *Entwicklungsauftrag*, the German for 'development instruction').

The so-called 'Type 29' (the internal Volkswagenwerk name for the new VW Transporter) took shape during 1949, with the first prototypes being built on the Beetle chassis. Unfortunately, though, early tests showed that a commercially used van, built up on a separate chassis, did not work. All prototypes had to be changed into a self-supporting body shell, supported by two frame side rails. The initial engine and axles of the Beetle were used. The engine had a displacement of 1131cc and a power of 23bhp (3,300rpm). The payload of the Type 29 was about 750kg.

In November 1949, Nordhoff was able to make a very successful presentation of four VW Transporters to the press. As a result of their favourable reception, more Type 29 Transporters were

released in February 1950. Mass production started on 8 March 1950 with ten vehicles per day. The only thing missing was a real name for the new Volkswagen Transporter, all suggestions having been rejected by the patent office. Even without a 'real' name, however, the vehicle turned out to be the forerunner of all modern cargo or passenger vans.

Eventually, the works names 'Type 29' and, later, 'Type 2' or 'VW Transporter', all stayed in use. The Buses of the second generation were also called 'Bay Window Buses', but right up until today the Bus is more commonly referred to as the 'VW Bus', or, more affectionately, 'Bulli'.

A Move to Hannover

The maximum capacity of the production in Wolfsburg was eighty VW Transporters per day. This was not enough to satisfy the enormous demand that resulted from the economic boom following the Second World War in Germany and other European countries.

Nordhoff decided to build a factory solely for commercial vehicles and began to look around for the ideal location. The new factory would need good motorway connections, and to be close to a port and to the existing factory in Wolfsburg, and the Volkswagenwerk management quickly settled on Hannover. On 1 March 1955, Heinrich Nordhoff laid the first foundation stone and the first VW Transporter left the new factory just over a year later, on 8 March 1956. Mass production began on 20 April of the same year.

There was also a significant demand for engines within Volkswagenwerk, so Nordhoff decided to produce them in Hannover too. Engine production began on 11 November 1958, alongside the Transporter's continuing boom all over the world. In 1962, just twelve years after

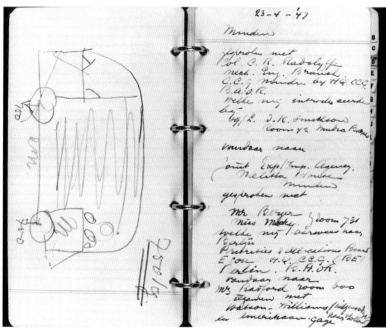

1947: sketch by Ben Pon.

1949: the first VW Transporter.

1956: The new Hannover factory.

its introduction, the millionth T1 left the Hannover factory.

THE EVOLUTION OF THE T2

As the VW Transporter of the first generation began to look a little dated, Volkswagenwerk thought about a successor to the T1. The first prototype to follow, in 1960, was called 'EA 114'. For various reasons, Heinrich Nordhoff decided to discontinue any further development at the time, but three years later the project had a new beginning. The board of VW charged Gustav Mayer, head of the development department for light commercial vehicles at the time, to lead a thorough reworking of the T1.

The development of the second-generation Transporter took barely three years, with the green light being given around the end of 1964/beginning of 1965. With the help of testing engineers from former German car manufacturer Borgward (Bremen), and design engineers borrowed from Porsche, Mayer set about the difficult task of designing and developing a new generation of the Bus within a relatively short time frame. As time pressed on, the tests were made on an intensified testing ground by the time-lapse method; in this kind of testing, each driven kilometre represents 5km under 'normal' conditions.

During the development of the vehicle, the VW designers had to solve many problems, both small and significant. The body of the new-generation Transporter failed to last through the test cycle and had to be entirely reworked. The solution was a self-supporting body, consisting of an extra inner skin of metal sheet. This double-walled construction solved the strength problems, and allowed even the braces between every window at both sides of the Bus, taken from the T1, to be removed. This resulted in larger side windows. Test drives with the optimized prototypes were continued and the team come closer to the completion of the new T2.

In order to test the durability of the vehicle under extreme climatic conditions, the Transporter was transferred to the north of Sweden for the so-called 'winter try out'. The tests for heat resistance were done in South Africa. Both took place in 1966.

Even after volume production began, in the summer of 1967, the team

The new VW T2.

continued to develop and improve the T2. In 1969, five Bay Window Buses with a fully galvanized body shell were completed for testing purposes. However, the costs for serial production of these Buses was too high, and mass production was not carried out.

A YEAR OF CHANGES

On 12 April 1968, the general director of Volkswagenwerk Heinz Heinrich Nordhoff died after a long illness. Largely due to his efforts, Volkswagenwerk AG had become a car manufacturer with an international reputation. He was succeeded as general director by Kurt Lotz.

There was much sadness among the Volkswagenwerk employees at the loss of Nordhoff. His funeral took place on 15 May 1968 in the 'Volkswagen-Town' Wolfsburg. So that an enormous crowd of people could pay their respects, the

Funeral march through the VW factory.

T2 Pick-Up carrying Nordhoff's coffin.

coffin was carried through the streets of Wolfsburg and to the factory on the back of a black T2a Pick-Up without a cabin roof.

First Model Change

Volkswagenwerk AG was still young, but it was about to initiate its first model change. Looking towards the beginning of the model year 1968, production of the second-generation VW Transporter began (in the summer of 1967) in the Hannover factory.

The Kombi, Microbus, Microbus L, Panelvan, and single- and double-cab Pick-Up were available right from the beginning of production. In the August 1967 brochure, which first introduced the Bay Window to the public, the Microbus was referred to as the 'Clipper' and the Deluxe version 'Clipper L'. In the end, Volkswagen was not allowed to use the name since it was registered for a type of aircraft by Pan Am airline. Instead, Volkswagen had to use less inspirational names such as VW-Kleinbus or VW-Personentransporter. However, the name 'Clipper' is still used by many Bus enthusiasts for the T2a Microbus.

Many innovations and improvements were made to the new Volkswagen Transporter compared with the Split Window Bus. For a start, it grew in length by 160mm to 4,420mm, with the result that the volume of the load compartment increased from 4.8 cubic metres to 5 cubic metres. The construction of the body was also changed. The evolution from the T1 into the new generation involved, among other developments, the introduction of a double-jointed rear axle, replacing the swing axle of the T1. Another innovation was the use of double-walled metal sheets on the car body to improve the body's stiffness.

All Buses of the second generation received a large one-piece wrap-around

T2: first Transporters leaving the factory.

windscreen, replacing the twin windscreens of the T1 and inspiring the nickname 'Bay Window'. In addition, optional winding windows in the cabin doors and larger side windows were available.

A more powerful engine, with 47bhp at 4,000rpm, was introduced. The displacement performance was enlarged, from 1493 to 1570cc. The cooling of the engine was guaranteed by air-intake louvres on each side in the back of the Bus, behind the rear side windows.

The load compartment and the cabin were also rearranged. The T2 was equipped with a completely redesigned dashboard with padded edges and three separate instruments: fuel tank capacity display, speedometer and clock (optional extra). Furthermore, there were plastic control knobs marked with symbols, two external mirrors, a new ventilation system with ventilation grilles under the windscreen and adjustable fresh air vents inside, a safety-type ashtray, a grab handle for passengers, an adjustable front seat and a new handbrake lever under the dashboard.

The sliding door, an optional extra on the T1, was now fitted as standard. Also standard, from April 1968 for the special 'Clipper' model, was the metal sun-roof, which now made a decent modern successor of the well-known folding sunroof of the Split Window Deluxe 'Samba' model.

Already familiar in the shipbuilding industry, fibreglass was introduced at Volkswagen for the roof of the T2 high-roof Panelvan. Compared to the preceding model, a huge reduction of weight could be realized by introducing this new and non-rusting material. The high-roof tops were manufactured exclusively by a French manufacturer for Volkswagen.

During this time, Volkswagen was also pursuing the idea of using similar parts; for example, the ashtray of the Bay Window Bus belonged to the Type 3 and the headlamps to the Beetle.

Expanding Capacity

The success of the second-generation Bus was overwhelming and in 1968 the two-millionth VW Transporter left the Hannover factory. It was a Titian Red-coloured T2a Clipper with a Cloud White roof, donated to the German charity project 'Aktion Sorgenkind'.

The Hannover factory was unable to satisfy the enormous demand from the US market on its own, so Volkswagen decided to give some of the assembly work to the factory in Emden, a harbour city located in the very north-west of Germany. Production began in December 1967. Models for the US market that involved a high expenditure of work, such as Kombis, Microbuses and Microbuses L, were assembled there. The advantages were obvious: the US market could be served very quickly by the nearby seaport and the final assembly line in Hannover – formerly a bottleneck – was unburdened. The standard models, such as the Panelvan,

T2: the new driver's place.

1968: 2 million VW Transporters.

'Basic-Transporter' for developing countries.

T2a: Crash test.

Pick-Up and double-cab Pick-Up, continued to be produced in Hannover.

The success of the second generation lead to the highest-ever export rate of Transporters, even compared with today. In 1970, 72,515 Bay Window Buses were exported to the US market alone and the three-millionth VW Transporter left the production line on 3 September 1971. In the year 1972, a record 294,932 Bay Windows were produced in Hannover and Emden.

In April 1973 VW stopped production at Emden. One of the reasons for this move was the first oil crisis in the same year and the subsequent economic recession in Germany. All capacities were removed to Hannover, where, in 1973, 234,788 VW Transporters were built.

In 1973 VW introduced the 'Basic Transporter', a very simple and cheap commercially used vehicle specifically designed for developing countries. This odd-looking vehicle, constructed from different parts and the 1600cc engine from the Volkswagen programme, disposed of a front drive element. Low demand and a relatively high price meant that this project was a failure for Volkswagen.

VEHICLE SAFETY

The first-generation Volkswagen Transporter was supposed to fulfil the simple tasks of a basic utility vehicle, providing enough space to move people and products around, while remaining affordable. The demands on the second generation were more than this. As the amount of traffic increased on the roads, safety features became more and more important.

Volkswagen quality is well known: all new safety features were substantially tested in simulations or crash tests before they became part of the volume production. From August 1969, in the event of a head-on accident, the new safety steering column would snap at its rated break point, to reduce the risk of the driver getting injured.

The T2 also got a double-jointed rear axle as standard equipment, providing the Bus with the comfort of a passenger car. In 1971, the T2 was fitted with larger rear lights replacing the small ones and, after the factory holidays in 1972, all Buses got new bumpers with a deformable area at the front.

T2b Panelvan prototype for the USA.

prototypes *and* unique models

2

In the automobile industry prototypes are the very first models of a vehicle, the master for series production. Very often the decision-makers have a prototype redeveloped over and over again, before they finally accept the result. Some of the prototype Buses were really bizarre specimens, but unfortunately only a small number have survived. This chapter covers some of the known and unknown prototypes of the T2.

T2 WITH FOUR-WHEEL DRIVE

Without the approval or knowledge of the former board members of Volkswagen, two passionate VW engineers, Gustav Mayer (known as 'Transporter Mayer') and Henning Duckstein, secretly developed an allroad vehicle based on the VW T2. This unofficial project was referred to internally as EA 456/01. First tests were made in the Sahara desert in 1975/76 with a red and white T2b Kombi.

The test drives began on 25 December 1975. Starting the trip in Tunis, via El-Oued in Algeria, the route lead to the Grand Erg, a type of desert with impressively high dunes (over 400m high), ending in Hassi Messaoud. From there they came back to Tunis, and then shipped the Bus to Genoa in Italy. The extended try-out, over 800km, and difficult circumstances were mastered by the T2 without any problem.

Unfortunately, the development of the T2-Allroad was unofficial and occurred at the end of the T2's production span. The resultant Bus tested in the Sahara desert remained one of five prototype allroad vehicles that never went into series production. However, VW would go on to use the knowledge they had gained from this inventive project, building an allroad vehicle in the third Transporter generation.

T2b four-wheel drive.

Four-wheel drive, exhaust pipe in bumper.

After some extensive research, two four-wheel-drive Buses based on the T2 have been discovered. One is exhibited in the VW AutoMuseum in Wolfsburg, while the other is owned by a German private collector.

The T2-Allroad had a standard 50hp engine, and a number of distinguishing features, as follows:

- sheet metal tub and protecting runner under the front power train;
- four-gear transmission (the gearshift pattern corresponding with the standard fittings);
- torque converter;
- the cardan shaft to the modified rear axle transmission was placed in the front;
- the front wheels had a lockable drive element;
- 16in wheels;
- the exhaust pipe was integrated in the bumper;
- power lock differential;
- the standard front axle suspension was modified;
- wade depth of about 500mm;
- three extra instruments in the dashboard: oil pressure switch, tachometer, differential oil pressure switch.

Front view (top) and back view (above) of the T2b 'Safari'.

Fuel consumption (measured on the later prototype with 2000cc-carburettor engine) was 13–16l/100km and maximum speed was 115–120km/h. Its climbing ability (max.) was 77–94 per cent at 1,900kg gross weight, and 63–78 per cent at 2,300kg gross weight.

Over the years, five prototypes – three Kombis and two Westfalia Campers with a pop-up roof – were built. They had the following German licence plates:

T2b Kombi (Type 22): WOB-VK 25 (red/white); WOB-VM2 (olive green); BS-JT 941 (red/white)
T2b Camper (Type 239): WOB-VM89 (ivory); WOB-VA 73 (ivory)

In the years that followed, the T2-Allroad was gradually improved step by step, gaining a 2000cc-carburettor engine.

T2 KOMBI 'SAFARI'

Following the four-wheel-drive prototypes, the sales department ordered a new study of a T2 'Safari' from the

Interior: perforated sheet metal.

Interior: Safari model with spade.

development department. A prototype based on a T2b Kombi was assembled, featuring many details that were not available for the standard models. In the front, this prototype was fitted out with black lamp rings, bared head and fog lights. An electric cable winch was attached over the front bumper, and the searchlight that was familiar on the Ambulance was also included. Lateral guide rails and plastic casing on the wheel housing completed the look.

Like a 'standard', this prototype had a black roof-rack, lamella windows in the sliding door and on the opposing side.

(These were initially used only on Camper Buses.) The windows in the back were made of clear plastic. On the back of the Bus the name 'Safari' was written.

The interior arrangement was very practical. Beside the sleeping bench, a foldable table was fixed on the inner body side. There were curtains at the windows. Some of these details were well known from the T2 Westfalia Campmobiles.

The Safari was equipped with two pieces of perforated sheet metal, which made it possible for the Bus to drive on sandy subsoil, or even through the

T2b Panelvan cargo compartment
laid out with carpet.

T2c Kombi VW do Brazil.
ABOVE: *Front view.* RIGHT: *Interior layout.*
BELOW: *Back view.* BOTTOM: *Cabin layout.*

desert. A spade was also part of the Safari's equipment.

C-rails on the inner body side and the partitioning wall behind the driver's seat made it possible to fix heavy loads.

T2B PANELVAN USA

The T2 shown on page 5 is a curious-looking Bay Window Bus based on a US version of the Panelvan. Completely coated in a gold metallic paint, this Bay Window has a round window on each rear outer body side, borrowed from the shipbuilding industry. The interior of the cargo compartment, including the floor, the inner body sides, the inner roof and sliding door, were covered with brown carpet.

KOMBI VW DO BRASIL

This Brazilian Kombi de luxe (*see* right) belongs to the Wolfsburg Stiftung Auto-Museum Volkswagen collection. It is a 1998 T2 7-Seater 'Kombi-Lotação' with a significant amount of non-serial equipment, and the following features:

- bi-colour lacquering, with the main body in light green metallic, and roof in white;
- steering wheel with the new VW logo;
- interior trim, dashboard and seats in light beige;
- leather upholstery;
- chrome T2a hubcaps;
- chrome bumpers;
- whitewall tyres.

T2 KOMBI 'VW DE MEXICO'

This prototype of a Bay Window Bus (*see* page 12) was a design model for a facelift of the Mexican T2 model. Note the front-turn signals right below the headlights – reminiscent of the T2a – as

Mexican T2 prototype 'facelift'.

1973: T2b open air.

well as the large rear-view mirrors and rectangular headlamps.

T2B OPEN-AIR BUS

For a very popular German television show called *Der Große Preis* Volkswagen produced a convertible-like Open-Air Bus, based on the T2b Kombi. Unusual were the small air-intake louvres in the back and the chequered seats. This Bus is now part of the collection of the Stiftung AutoMuseum Volkswagen, located in the VW factory in Kassel.

ALTERNATIVE DRIVE ELEMENTS

The oil crisis at the beginning of the 1970s, and the pressing shortage of non-renewable energy sources, forced VW to undertake research into alternative drive elements. Two sources of energy that were tested, among others, were gas and electricity. The Bus was used as a testing vehicle for such alternatives for one very simple reason: no other vehicle in the VW product range was spacious enough to accommodate the testing drive elements.

The electric-powered Bus was the only model to be built in a small-volume production. All other tested drive elements remained at testing level.

Electric Engine

The VW Transporter with an electric drive assembly was available as a Kombi (Type 23), Panelvan (Type 21) and Pick-Up (Type 26), and could be ordered at German Volkswagen dealers.

The electric engine was built by Siemens. The standard Bus was delivered

ABOVE: *T2b Pick-Up: manual battery change.*
ABOVE RIGHT: *T2b Panelvan: battery change.*

ABOVE: *Electric engine.*
RIGHT: *Technical drawing of the electro Pick-Up.*

VW Electromobil

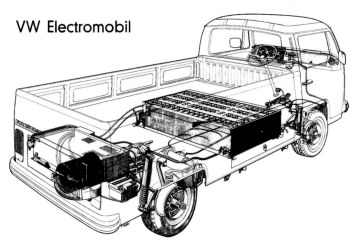

LEFT: T2a/b Pick-Up prototype.

ABOVE: Dashboard of an Electric Transporter.

Basic Specification of the Volkswagen Electric Transporter

Energy demand: 55kWh/100km

Range: 50 to 80km

Max. speed: 80km/h

Batteries: peak power 33kW (44hp),
permanent power 17kW (23hp)

Payload: 800kg

with a set of lead batteries (860kg), a battery charger in form of a cupboard with a high-voltage current connection and a rack with which to change the batteries. The batteries were located in the middle of the Bus for ease of access. Changing the batteries was also made easier on the Kombis and Panelvans by the presence of two sliding doors. The Pick-Ups were fitted out with two panel lids.

The maximum weight that could be carried was increased by specific shock absorbers.

Hybrid Engine

The VW Transporter equipped with the hybrid drive element had a standard combustion engine in the back. The concept involved the combination of an electric and a combustion engine. A hydrodynamic converter and an electro-pneumatic clutch connected the engine with the gearbox. In addition to this, eleven batteries were placed in the passenger compartment and the compartment right above the engine. When the batteries were charged, the driver was able to switch into electric mode, using the electric motor placed behind the driver's seat in the passenger compartment (*see below*). When the Bus did not use the entire power produced by the combustion engine, the batteries were charged, while driving.

Gas Turbine Engine

In 1972 Volkswagen build up a special testing vehicle, a T2a/b Microbus L, with gas turbine engine. This engine was similar to the jet engine used in aircraft, with a hot gas stream driving the impellers of

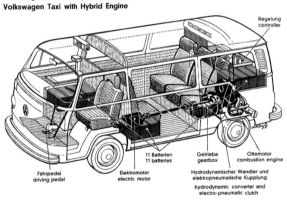

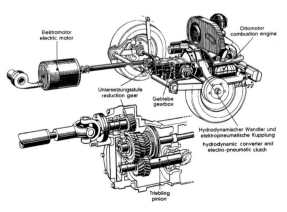

ABOVE: T2b Panelvan: enough space for goods.

RIGHT: Detailed description of the VW Transporter with Hybrid Engine.

TOP: *Side of the Gasturbine (SAV).*

MIDDLE LEFT: *Back of the Gasturbine with engine cutaway model (SAV).*

MIDDLE RIGHT: *Gas turbine engine.*

LEFT: *Adjusted engine lid (SAV).*

ABOVE: *Dashboard: additional instruments.*

a turbine shaft, which itself drove the Bus. The gas stream was made in a chamber by the combustion of gas.

The gas engine did not get much attention because of its low efficiency, and the project was abandoned by Volkswagen. The prototype (*see* above) is in the collection of the Stiftung Auto-Museum in Wolfsburg. It is a Microbus 8-seater former testing vehicle of the VW R & D department in Wolfsburg (internal testing number VR-1511). Conspicuous are the position of the front emblem, the non-serial colour combination of Red/Orange and the chrome bumpers.

2352111814

1972–79. Chassis number is stamped on upright metal profile on the left.

cracking the codes
vehicle identification

Most Buses built in Germany were fitted with two identification plates, containing information about model type and chassis number, as well as various other details. They are very useful for determining the original specification of a Transporter and for revealing build date, engine type, paint and trim finishing, as well as factory-fitted special equipment and the country to which the vehicle was delivered.

CHASSIS NUMBER OR VIN

The chassis number or VIN (Vehicle Identification Number) of a Bay Window is stamped on a metal profile in the engine compartment. On 1968–71 models, this is on the right side where the vehicle's bodywork borders with the engine's sheet metal. On 1972 and later models, the chassis number is stamped on an upright metal profile to the left of the

engine compartment, right behind the engine lid. This is also the place where the vehicle's bodywork and the engine's sheet metal meet.

Engine Number

The Bay Window was available with two different kinds of engine. The most common is the so-called Type 1 or 'upright' engine. The official reference for the other engine is 'Type 4', but its flat appearance inspired the nickname 'pancake engine'. The engine number shows the basic engine configuration and its serial number.

On Type 1 engines the number is stamped below the generator pedestal right underneath the text 'Zündfolge 1-4-3-2', which is German for 'order of ignition'.

On Buses with the Type 4 engine, the engine number can be read in two different places. The most visible spot is on the upper part of the fan housing. Theoretically, the fan housing could be swapped with another engine so the engine number is stamped in the crank case as well. This number is more reliable and can be found right behind the fan housing, where the left and right halves of the crank case meet. Usually, it is hard to read because of the layers of dust and dried-up oil that have collected there over the years.

For a complete list of the engines fitted in the Bay Window Bus, see Chapter 6.

1968–71. Chassis number is stamped next to the air filter stand, left of the battery.

Type 1 engine number is stamped on crankcase right below the generator/alternator pedestal.

Type 4 engine number is stamped on top of the fan housing (1) and on the crank case between the oil breather and the fan housing (2).

How to Read the Chassis Number

In the years 1968 and 1969, chassis numbers had nine digits – two digits for the model specification, one for the model year and six for the serial number. For example, the chassis number '219 092 212' denotes a VW Panelvan (21), produced in model year 1969 (9), and with the serial number 092 212.

From model years 1970–79, the chassis number contained ten digits – two digits for the model specification, one for the model year, an extra one to distinguish between 1960s and 1970s chassis numbers and six digits for the serial number. The number distinguishing between 1960s and 1970s chassis numbers was always a '2'. So, for example, the chassis number '2302 241 209' denotes a VW Kombi (23), produced in model year 1970 (0), with the number '2' denoting a 70s VIN, and a serial number of 241 209.

In the event that the factory ever ran out of serial numbers during a model year, the '2' would become a '3'. The serial number had six digits, so this would be necessary only if more than a million Transporters were built during one model year and, indeed, it only happened with the Beetle, which had a similar VIN system. The annual Transporter production was always between 150,000 to 280,000 vehicles a year.

CHASSIS PLATE

The chassis plate is found behind the passenger seat (for RHD vehicles, the driver's seat) in the cabin. The aluminium plate, fixed with rivets on the metal wall, displayed the word 'Typ', followed by the kind of Type 2 model involved. In some cases, a suffix provided extra information, for example, a chassis plate 'Typ 23/AD' denotes a VW Kombi with an AD engine (1600cc).

The system varied depending on the market. The chassis plate on Italian Buses, for example, displayed the engine type as well.

Below the Bus type number, the text 'Heizg.Typ 2' stands for the German term 'Heizung Typ 2', which refers to the type of heater used in the Type 2. On a standard Transporter fresh air was warmed up by being blown alongside the hot exhaust pipes. This happened in the heater boxes. There were two different types of heater box, those of the Type 1 engine (1300 and 1600cc) and those fitted on Type 4 engines (1700, 1800 and 2000cc).

Heater boxes were tested by the German authorities and given a certificate number, which is printed on the plate after the heater type number. There are two different certificate numbers:

255 A Prüfz. – S45
255 B Prüfz. – S111

S45 is the certificate number for Type 1 engines (1300 and 1600cc). The Type 4 heater boxes were given certificate number S111 (1700, 1800 and 2000cc).

'Fahrgest.-Nr.' is the German abbreviation for *Fahrgestellnummer*, which means 'chassis number' (known as 'VIN' in the USA).

Chassis plate is fitted behind passenger seat (RHD: driver's seat).

The most common type numbers	

Type	Description
21	Panelvan
21-515	Panelvan – High-roof (M515)
21F	Panelvan – Fire truck
22	Microbus
23	Kombi
23-517	Kombi – Westfalia Campmobile (M517)
24	Microbus Deluxe
26	Pick-Up (single-cab only; from 1977 onwards, all Pick-Up models)
26-16	Crew-cab Pick-Up (1968–76)
26-201	Pick-Up with enlarged wooden platform (1968–76)(M201)
27	Ambulance
28	Microbus – Seven-seater

'Zul. Gesamtgew. kg' is the maximum total weight of the Bus in kilograms.

'Zul. Achslast kg' is the maximum axle load in kilograms with the value after 'vorn' for the front axle and 'hinten' for the rear axle.

'Baujahr' stands for the year of manufacture although the spot was always left blank.

NOTE: Buses made for certain export markets or assembled overseas might have a different chassis plate.

M-PLATE

In 1958 a metal plate with production codes was introduced on the Type 2. Among VW Bus enthusiasts, this plate is commonly known as the 'M-plate', the

Chassis plate for UK and Ireland (M61).

Chassis plate on Australian CKD vehicle (GE).

Plates from a 1978 CKD Bus with chassis number 2182 008 506 (TvW).

Chassis plate on South African CKD vehicle.

'M' referring to the German word *Mehrausstattung*, which means 'optional extra'. The optional extras are printed on the plate in codes, called 'M-codes', but more details than that are covered, including paint and interior colours, destination (if built for export), engine and transmission type and planned production date.

In the Bay Window the M-plate is riveted to the metal partition behind the driver's seat (the passenger seat on RHD vehicles). From model year 1977 onwards the plate is fixed under the dashboard, on top of the fresh-air pipe, left of the fuse box.

On Buses from before 1976 a silver adhesive sticker was located below the M-plate, displaying the name of the colour and the paint code, beginning with an 'L'. The labels were printed on paper, so in many cases they have not survived. All Buses with colours from the regular sales programme had this sticker. From model year 1978 on also the vehicles with special paint colours had a sticker with colour name and L-code.

MISSING PLATES

Buses assembled in factories overseas do not have an M-plate. The holes are there but, for some unknown reason, the plates were never fitted. Most of the car parts were produced in Germany and then shipped to the overseas factory where the vehicles were assembled, which is probably why the holes for the plate are there.

Some German-assembled Buses came without the chassis plate. This was done for certain export markets in the late 1970s. This could be option M912 or it could be the case, as in the USA and Canada, that the chassis plate was replaced by a sticker in the door jam.

HOW TO READ THE M-PLATE

In the first two years of the Bay Window, the M-plate layout of the Split Window Bus was used. From 1970 onwards the layout was different and a code for production planning was added. This new code started with a 7 in most cases. It was used as a temporary serial number in the factory to determine the order of vehicles on the production line.

In some Buses the codes on the first line of the M-plate are followed by an 'E',

1968–76. M-plate is fixed behind driver's seat (RHD: passenger seat).

1977–79. M-plate is fixed left of fuse box on top of fresh-air duct.

denoting a Bus that was built in Emden. This happened in the period December 1967 to April 1973, when the factory in Hannover had more work than it could handle.

The second line is left blank if all M-codes fit on the third line.

Scheduled Production Date

The date printed on the plate is the scheduled production date and usually the actual production date was not far off this. In 1969 VW changed the system for encrypting the date.

The old system is the way of dating as used on the Split Window Buses: two digits for the day, and one for the month. For months January until September, '1' to '9' were used. For October, November and December the letters 'O', 'N' and 'D' were used. The year of manufacture can be determined from the model year. A model year always starts in the August before the beginning of the actual calendar year. For example, a Bus built in August 1969 is actually from model year 1970. It is possible to get a hint from the chassis number whether it was an early Bus for that model year or a late one. The serial number (last six digits) would always start at 000001 in August and ended around 200,000 depending on the scale of production at the time.

On 17 March 1969 the dating system was changed, around chassis number 219151000. From this day on, week and

Additional stickers for the US market.

1968–1969

```
DD D  (E)
MMM  MMM  MMM  MMM  MMM
YZ  MMM  MMM  MMM  MMM  MMM
XX  TTTT  PPPPUU  CCCCCCC
```

1970–1979

```
CC  CCC  CCC  (E)
MMM  MMM  MMM  MMM  MMM
PPPPUU  MMM  MMM  MMM  MMM
DD D  VVVV  XX  TTTT  YZ
```

DD D = scheduled production date
(E) = an 'E' here denotes a Bus built in Emden
YZ = aggregate code:, engine (Y) and gearbox (Z)
MMM = M-code or group code
XX = destination code
TTTT = model code
PPPPUU = paint (P) and interior (U) codes
CCCCCCC = chassis number
VVVV = code used for production planning

day numbers were used. The week number represents the number of the week in a calendar year. The day number is the number of the day in the week ('1' to '6' for Monday to Saturday).

Clearly, interpreting the date encryption is not very easy without an old calendar. The table on page 19 gives all the dates for the first day (Monday) of every week from March 1969, when this dating system was introduced, until July 1979, when the last German Bay Window was made.

Aggregate Code

The aggregate code comprises the engine and transmission codes. The first digit is for the engine type and the second for the transmission. For more on these, *see* Chapter 6.

M-Codes

The M-codes ('M' from the German *Mehr- und Minderausstattung*, which means 'more or lesser equipment') clarify the way in which the Transporter is different from the standard model. Each M-code consists of three numbers, often mentioned in VW literature with the letter 'M' in front of them. M-codes represent extra equipment ordered at the dealer, requirements for certain export markets or items that needed to be left out, either to save costs or because of legal requirements. In some cases, the code represents a whole range of optional extras.

For a list of the M-codes, *see* Chapter 7. A very small number of Buses came without M-codes.

Destination Code

The destination is given in either numbers or letters. Buses produced before 17 March 1969 (chassis no. 219151000) might have an empty spot instead of the destination code, in that case the Bus was a vehicle for the German market. After this date a number is shown if the Bus was destined for West Germany. Letters stand for an export destination.

For a list of all the destination codes, *see* Chapter 9.

Model Code

The model code describes what the model looked like in its basic configuration, without any M-specifications. The model number always starts with a '2', for 'VW Type 2'. The second digit refers to body type: '1' for the Panelvan, '2' and '4' for the Microbus, '3' for the Kombi, '6' for the Pick-Up and '7' for the Ambulance. The first two digits are actually closely related to the 'type' specification on the chassis plate. If the third digit is an odd number it was a left-hand-drive vehicle, an even number indicated a right-hand-drive vehicle. The fourth number tells if there is an important M-code on the Bus related to the interior, for example, a fire-brigade conversion or an M-code specifying the number of seats in the back.

For more information about this, *see* Chapter 6.

Paint and Interior Code

The paint and interior are described on the M-plate in three separate pairs of digits. The first two digits represent the colour used for the lower part of the Bus, the second the paint colour for the upper part of the body. The border between these colours is the raingutter on 1968–70 models; on 1971–79 models it is the lower part of the belt line, about 10cm (4in) below the window seals. The last two numbers represent the interior colour and material that was used.

If a special colour was used or a specially ordered paint job was applied, the code must be read in another way. In these cases, the first digit is a '5' or a '9'. For detailed information on this subject, *see* Chapter 8.

Chassis Number

The chassis number on the M-plate is the full chassis number without the first two digits that specify the model number. For example, if the full chassis number is 21909212, then the chassis number on the M-plate will read 9092212, omitting the '21' for Panelvan.

WORKING OUT EXACT DATES

The table shows all the week and day numbers as they were printed on the M-plate from around chassis no. 219 151 000. To calculate the date mentioned on the plate, first, determine the model year of the Bus by looking at the chassis number (third digit of the full chassis number or the first digit of the chassis number as it is printed on the M-plate). Referring to model year and week number, find the exact date of the first day in the table. The date is the Monday of that week.

For example, to find the date of week 43, day 3 of model year 1978, you need to determine that the Monday of that week was 24/10/1977, so day 3 (Wednesday) was 26/10/1977.

EXAMPLE OF HOW TO READ A CHASSIS PLATE AND M-PLATE

The chassis plate and M-plate shown below were taken from the same vehicle, a VW Kombi with the chassis number 2362 129 476. The maximum gross weight is 2,300kg, and the maximum axle loads are 1,010kg on the front and 1,300kg on the rear axle. The codes may be read as follows:

Standard chassis plate.

M-plate example (1970–79 layout).

- 62 129 476 = chassis number without two-digit model number in front. '6' stands for model year 1976 and 129476 is the serial number;
- 508 = M-code for ventilation window in sliding door and in all windows opposite the sliding door in the passenger compartment;
- 511 = M-code for padded dashboard;
- 697 = M-code for Continental tyres;
- E6E677 = paint and interior code: E6 for lower half in Chrome Yellow; E6 for upper half in Chrome Yellow; 77 for Canyon Brown interior;
- B30 = group code representing: M050, hand brake and dual circuit control light; M123, suppression equipment; M506, brake servo; M507, ventilation windows in cabin doors; M528, convex rear view mirror (right);
- 060 = M-code for petrol heater;
- 171 = M-code for tubeless textile or steel-ply tyres;
- 504 = M-code for fresh-air duct to cargo compartment
- 18 2 = planned production date of week 18, day 2 (Tuesday) (27 April 1976);
- 7288 = number for production planning (temporary serial number);
- HO = destination code for the Netherlands;
- 2312 = model code representing: 23, VW Kombi; 1, LHD, sliding door right; 2, six seating places in rear (M13);
- 11 = aggregate code representing: 1, Type 1 engine (1600cc); 1, manual gearbox, 4-speed.

Model year 1969
Chassis nos. 219 151 000–219 300 000

Week	Day 1	Week	Day 1	Week	Day 1
12	17.03.69	17	21.04.69	22	26.05.69
13	24.03.69	18	28.04.69	23	02.06.69
14	31.03.69	19	05.05.69	24	09.06.69
15	07.04.69	20	12.05.69	25	16.06.69
16	14.04.69	21	19.05.69	26	23.06.69

Model year 1970
Chassis nos. 2102 000 001–2102 248 837

Week	Day 1	Week	Day 1	Week	Day 1
29	14.07.69	47	17.11.69	13	23.03.70
30	21.07.69	48	24.11.69	14	30.03.70
31	28.07.69	49	01.12.69	15	06.04.70
32	04.08.69	50	08.12.69	16	13.04.70
33	11.08.69	51	15.12.69	17	20.04.70
34	18.08.69	52	22.12.69	18	27.04.70
35	25.08.69	01	29.12.69	19	04.05.70
36	01.09.69	02	05.01.70	20	11.05.70
37	08.09.69	03	12.01.70	21	18.05.70
38	15.09.69	04	19.01.70	22	25.05.70
39	22.09.69	05	26.01.70	23	01.06.70
40	29.09.69	06	02.02.70	24	08.06.70
41	06.10.69	07	09.02.70	25	15.06.70
42	13.10.69	08	16.02.70	26	22.06.70
43	20.10.69	09	23.02.70	27	29.06.70
44	27.10.69	10	02.03.70	28	06.07.70
45	03.11.69	11	09.03.70		
46	10.11.69	12	16.03.70		

Model year 1971
Chassis nos. 2112 000 001–2112 300 000

Week	Day 1	Week	Day 1	Week	Day 1
32	03.08.70	50	07.12.70	15	12.04.71
33	10.08.70	51	14.12.70	16	19.04.71
34	17.08.70	52	21.12.70	17	26.04.71
35	24.08.70	53	28.12.70	18	03.05.71
36	31.08.70	01	04.01.71	19	10.05.71
37	07.09.70	02	11.01.71	20	17.05.71
38	14.09.70	03	18.01.71	21	24.05.71
39	21.09.70	04	25.01.71	22	31.05.71
40	28.09.70	05	01.02.71	23	07.06.71
41	05.10.70	06	08.02.71	24	14.06.71
42	12.10.70	07	15.02.71	25	21.06.71
43	19.10.70	08	22.02.71	26	28.06.71
44	26.10.70	09	01.03.71	27	05.07.71
45	02.11.70	10	08.03.71	28	12.07.71
46	09.11.70	11	15.03.71	29	19.07.71
47	16.11.70	12	22.03.71	30	26.07.71
48	23.11.70	13	29.03.71	31	02.08.71
49	30.11.70	14	05.04.71		

Model year 1972
Chassis nos. 2122 000 001–2122 300 000

Week	Day 1	Week	Day 1	Week	Day 1
34	23.08.71	38	20.09.71	42	18.10.71
35	30.08.71	39	27.09.71	43	25.10.71
36	06.09.71	40	04.10.71	44	01.11.71
37	13.09.71	41	11.10.71	45	08.11.71
46	15.11.71	08	21.02.72	22	29.05.72
47	22.11.71	09	28.02.72	23	05.06.72
48	29.11.71	10	06.03.72	24	12.06.72
49	06.12.71	11	13.03.72	25	19.06.72
50	13.12.71	12	20.03.72	26	26.06.72
51	20.12.71	13	27.03.72	27	03.07.72
52	27.12.71	14	03.04.72	28	10.07.72
01	03.01.72	15	10.04.72	29	17.07.72
02	10.01.72	16	17.04.72	30	24.07.72
03	17.01.72	17	24.04.72	31	31.07.72
04	24.01.72	18	01.05.72		
05	31.01.72	19	08.05.72		
06	07.02.72	20	15.05.72		
07	14.02.72	21	22.05.72		

Model year 1973
Chassis nos. 2132 000 001–2132 300 000

Week	Day 1	Week	Day 1	Week	Day 1
34	21.08.72	52	25.12.72	18	30.04.73
35	28.08.72	01	01.01.73	19	07.05.73
36	04.09.72	02	08.01.73	20	14.05.73
37	11.09.72	03	15.01.73	21	21.05.73
38	18.09.72	04	22.01.73	22	28.05.73
39	25.09.72	05	29.01.73	23	04.06.73
40	02.10.72	06	05.02.73	24	11.06.73
41	09.10.72	07	12.02.73	25	18.06.73
42	16.10.72	08	19.02.73	26	25.06.73
43	23.10.72	09	26.02.73	27	02.07.73
44	30.10.72	10	05.03.73	28	09.07.73
45	06.11.72	11	12.03.73	29	16.07.73
46	13.11.72	12	19.03.73	30	23.07.73
47	20.11.72	13	26.03.73		
48	27.11.72	14	02.04.73		
49	04.12.72	15	09.04.73		
50	11.12.72	16	16.04.73		
51	18.12.72	17	23.04.73		

Model year 1974
Chassis nos. 2142 000 001–2142 300 000

Week	Day 1	Week	Day 1	Week	Day 1
33	13.08.73	51	17.12.73	17	22.04.74
34	20.08.73	52	24.12.73	18	29.04.74
35	27.08.73	01	31.12.73	19	06.05.74
36	03.09.73	02	07.01.74	20	13.05.74
37	10.09.73	03	14.01.74	21	20.05.74
38	17.09.73	04	21.01.74	22	27.05.74
39	24.09.73	05	28.01.74	23	03.06.74
40	01.10.73	06	04.02.74	24	10.06.74
41	01.08.73	07	11.02.74	25	17.06.74
42	15.10.73	08	18.02.74	26	24.06.74
43	22.10.73	09	25.02.74	27	01.07.74
44	29.10.73	10	04.03.74	28	08.07.74
45	05.11.73	11	11.03.74	29	15.07.74
46	12.11.73	12	18.03.74	30	22.07.74
47	19.12.73	13	25.03.74		
48	26.11.73	14	01.04.74		
49	03.12.73	15	08.04.74		
50	10.12.73	16	15.04.74		

(continued overleaf)

Model year 1975
Chassis nos. 2152 000 001–2152 300 000

Week	Day 1	Week	Day 1	Week	Day 1
33	12.08.74	51	16.12.74	17	21.04.75
34	19.08.74	52	23.12.74	18	28.04.75
35	26.08.74	01	30.12.74	19	05.05.75
36	02.09.74	02	06.01.75	20	12.05.75
37	09.09.74	03	13.01.75	21	19.05.75
38	16.09.74	04	20.01.75	22	26.05.75
39	23.09.74	05	27.01.75	23	02.06.75
40	30.09.74	06	03.02.75	24	09.06.75
41	07.10.74	07	10.02.75	25	16.06.75
42	14.10.74	08	17.02.75	26	23.06.75
43	21.10.74	09	24.02.75	27	30.06.75
44	28.10.74	10	03.03.75		
45	04.11.74	11	10.03.75		
46	11.11.74	12	17.03.75		
47	18.11.74	13	24.03.75		
48	25.11.74	14	31.03.75		
49	02.12.74	15	07.04.75		
50	09.12.74	16	14.04.75		

Model year 1976
Chassis nos. 2162 000 001–2162 300 000

Week	Day 1	Week	Day 1	Week	Day 1
30	21.07.75	48	24.11.75	14	29.03.76
31	28.07.75	49	01.12.75	15	05.04.76
32	04.08.75	50	08.12.75	16	12.04.76
33	11.08.75	51	15.12.75	17	19.04.76
34	18.08.75	52	22.12.75	18	26.04.76
35	25.08.75	01	29.12.75	19	03.05.76
36	01.09.75	02	05.01.76	20	10.05.76
37	08.09.75	03	12.01.76	21	17.05.76
38	15.09.75	04	19.01.76	22	24.05.76
39	22.09.75	05	26.01.76	23	31.05.76
40	29.09.75	06	02.02.76	24	07.06.76
41	06.10.75	07	09.02.76	25	14.06.76
42	13.10.75	08	16.02.76		
43	20.10.75	09	23.02.76		
44	27.10.75	10	01.03.76		
45	03.11.75	11	08.03.76		
46	10.11.75	12	15.03.76		
47	17.11.75	13	22.03.76		

Model year 1977
Chassis nos. 2172 000 001–2172 300 000

Week	Day 1	Week	Day 1	Week	Day 1
28	05.07.76	41	04.10.76	01	03.01.77
29	12.07.76	42	11.10.76	02	10.01.77
30	19.07.76	43	18.10.76	03	17.01.77
31	26.07.76	44	25.10.76	04	24.01.77
32	02.08.76	45	01.11.76	05	31.01.77
33	09.08.76	46	08.11.76	06	07.02.77
34	16.08.76	47	15.11.76	07	14.02.77
35	23.08.76	48	22.11.76	08	21.02.77
36	30.08.76	49	29.11.76	09	28.02.77
37	06.09.76	50	06.12.76	10	07.03.77
38	13.09.76	51	13.12.76	11	14.03.77
39	20.09.76	52	20.12.76	12	21.03.77
40	27.09.76	53	27.12.76	13	28.03.77
14	04.04.77	19	09.05.77	24	13.06.77
15	11.04.77	20	16.05.77	25	20.06.77
16	18.04.77	21	23.05.77	26	27.06.77
17	25.04.77	22	30.05.77		
18	02.05.77	23	06.06.77		

Model year 1978
Chassis nos. 2182 000 001–2182 300 000

Week	Day 1	Week	Day 1	Week	Day 1
30	25.07.77	48	28.11.77	14	03.04.78
31	01.08.77	49	05.12.77	15	10.04.78
32	08.08.77	50	12.12.77	16	17.04.78
33	15.08.77	51	19.12.77	17	24.04.78
34	22.08.77	52	26.12.77	18	01.05.78
35	29.08.77	01	02.01.78	19	08.05.78
36	05.09.77	02	09.01.78	20	15.05.78
37	12.09.77	03	16.01.78	21	22.05.78
38	19.09.77	04	23.01.78	22	29.05.78
39	26.09.77	05	30.01.78	23	05.06.78
40	03.10.77	06	06.02.78	24	12.06.78
41	10.10.77	07	13.02.78	25	19.06.78
42	17.10.77	08	20.02.78	26	26.06.78
43	24.10.77	09	27.02.78		
44	31.10.77	10	06.03.78		
45	07.11.77	11	13.03.78		
46	14.11.77	12	20.03.78		
47	21.11.77	13	27.03.78		

Model year 1979
Chassis nos. 2192 000 001–2192 153 964

Week	Day 1	Week	Day 1	Week	Day 1
28	10.07.78	46	13.11.78	12	19.03.79
29	17.07.78	47	20.11.78	13	26.03.79
30	24.07.78	48	27.11.78	14	02.04.79
31	31.07.78	49	04.12.78	15	09.04.79
32	07.08.78	50	11.12.78	16	16.04.79
33	14.08.78	51	18.12.78	17	23.04.79
34	21.08.78	52	25.12.78	18	30.04.79
35	28.08.78	01	01.01.79	19	07.05.79
36	04.09.78	02	08.01.79	20	14.05.79
37	11.09.78	03	15.01.79	21	21.05.79
38	18.09.78	04	22.01.79	22	28.05.79
39	25.09.78	05	29.01.79	23	04.06.79
40	02.10.78	06	05.02.79	24	11.06.79
41	09.10.78	07	12.02.79	25	18.06.79
42	16.10.78	08	19.02.79	26	25.06.79
43	23.10.78	09	26.02.79	27	02.07.79
44	30.10.78	10	05.03.79	28	09.07.79
45	06.11.78	11	12.03.79	29	16.07.79

The first model year of the T2 was 1968, the last 1979.

production survey

All Buses of the model years 1968–69 had a chassis number consisting of nine digits. The third digit (the first one on the M-plate) stands for the model year (for example, '9' for 1969).

The remaining digits show the serial number. Buses of the model years 1970–79 had a ten-digit chassis number meaning the same. For more details of this system, *see* Chapter 3.

The Volkswagen model year ran from August of the previous year to July the next year. For example, model year 1969 began in August 1968 and ended in July 1969.

Production details by model year

Year	Date	Model year	VIN Number	Year	Date	Model year	VIN Number
1967	1 August	1968	218 000 001	1976	31 July		216 2 300 000
	31 December		218 073 585		1 August	1977	217 2000 001
1968	31 July		218 202 251		31 December		217 2081 316
	1 August	1969	219 000 001	1977	31 July		217 2300 000
	31 December		219 098 974		1 August	1978	218 2000 001
1969	31 July		219 300 000		31 December		218 2072 273
	1 August	1970	210 2 000 001	1978	31 July		218 2300 000
	31 December		210 2106 747		1 August	1979	219 2000 001
1970	31 July		210 2 248 837		31 December		219 2073 637
	1 August	1971	211 2000 001	1979	31 October		219 2 153 964
	31 December		211 2114 988				
1971	31 July		211 2300 000				
	1 August	1972	211 2 000 001				
	31 December		212 2 088 996				
1972	31 July		212 2 300 000				
	1 August	1973	212 2 000 001				
	31 December		213 2 102 496				
1973	31 July		213 2 300 000				
	1 August	1974	213 2 000 001				
1974	31 July		214 2 300 000				
	1 August	1975	214 2 000 001				
	31 December		215 2 073 083				
1975	31 July		215 2 300 000				
	1 August	1976	215 2 000 001				
	31 December		216 2 077 675				

Counting point 8 in the production line (MS).

Production Numbers

Year	Production totals worldwide (including CKD)	Microbus	Kombi	Ambulance	Panelvan %	Double-cab Pick-Up	Pick-Up
1967*	162,741	22.0	29.1	0.4	27.8	5.2	15.5
1968	253,919	28.3	30.0	0.5	22.3	5.3	13.6
1969	273,134	26.3	31.8	0.5	22.4	6.2	12.8
1970	288,011	27.8	33.9	0.5	20.8	6.0	11.0
1971	277,503	29.9	34.7	0.6	19.1	5.9	9.8
1972	294,932	25.7	35.0	0.7	21.6	6.5	10.5
1973	289,022	23.7	35.7	0.8	23.1	6.3	10.4
1974	224,993	22.2	36.8	1.0	22.8	7.0	10.2
1975	227,087	18.2	40.0	1.1	24.7	6.9	9.1
1976	242,352	18.5	38.7	0.8	26.7	7.0	8.3
1977	208,615	23.6	34.3	0.9	24.9	7.5	8.8
1978	206,840	22.2	33.8	0.9	26.2	8.7	8.2
1979**	186,870	16.5	37.2	0.7	33.1	4.6	7.9

100. Volkswagen.

NOTES: * together with T1 (Split Window);
** together with T3 (Vanagon)

Notable Production Dates T2 (1967–79)

1967 August: Start of production in Hannover
December: Start of production at Emden

1968 5 February: 2,000,000th Transporter. Donated to the German charity organization Aktion Sorgenkind

1970 Highest export rate: 72,515 Transporters for the US market

1971 3 September: 3,000,000th Transporter

1972 259,101 Transporters produced in Emden and Hannover, the highest production number in one year until today

1973 234,788 Transporters produced in Hannover, the highest production rate record in the Hannover factory until today
April: End of production at Emden

1975 10 July: 4,000,000th Transporter

1979 End of production at Hannover (chassis no. 219 2 153 964)

LEFT: The last German T2, built in October 1979.
ABOVE: 60,000th VW for Belgium (SAV).

Body Shop

A *Welding the rear wheel arch.*

B *Setting in the doors.*

C *Welding the body shell.*

D *Body shell of a T2a/b (MS).*

E *The body shell going into the immersion bath.*

F *Setting in the partitioning wall.*

G *Welding.*

H *Production line in the body shop.*

Painting Bath

I *Preservation with wax.*

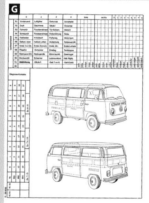

Production Line

A Setting in the front axle.

B Production of the T2a (MS).

C Production of the T2b.

D T2b High Roof Panelvan; VW 181.

E Counting point 8: the production is finished.

F Checking the front lights.

G Wagenprüfkarte (vehicle test record) for the T2. Every new Bus was tested and inspected before it left the factory.

1968–69 rotating light and siren switches.

specification detail changes

Most of the changes in the construction and features of the Bay Window Bus were made in August after the factory summer holidays, at the kick-off of the new model year.

NOTE: If the text or table refers to a specific year it always means the model year, unless a month or exact date is given, in which case it is the calendar year. Changes are listed chronologically according to the model year.

Engine-lid hinge

1968–76 engine-lid hinge.

Model year 1968
Chassis nos. 218 000 001–218 202 251

Date	Chassis no.	Change
08.67	218 000 001	Start of model year 1968: start of T2 production.
09.67		30 PICT-2 carb replaces 30 PICT-1 carb, engine nos. B0 019 736 and up (engines with M157 already had 30 PICT-2 carburettor).
02.68	218 098 285	Hazard light switch and relay changed; certain switch functions transferred from the relay to the switch.
	218 109 823	Brake backing plates front and rear got hole for inspecting brake-pad thickness. Rear brake backing plate and drum changed. Different design works better to keep dirt outside the drums.
04.68	218 133 164	Sliding roof introduced as optional extra (M560), standard on Microbus Deluxe (Type 24).
	218 135 858	Pistons changed (engine no. B0 091 149 and up).
05.68	218 160 611	Partition between fuel tank and engine compartment introduced.
05.68	218 163 486	Generator changed, technical specifications remain the same (engine no. B0 108 814 and up).

1977–79 engine-lid hinge.

Door handles

1968–71 rear hatch handle.

1972–74 rear hatch handle.

1975–79 rear hatch handle.

Model year 1969		
Chassis nos. 219 000 001–219 300 000		

Month	Chassis no.	Change
08.68	219 000 001	Start of model year 1969
		Engine: tumblers changed, cable for valve on warm-air inlet of air filter shortened (now 800mm instead of 815mm), fixed to valve with clamp, instead of being fixed with screw and bolt.
		Body: changes to cabin door, now lockable from the inside by operating a small handle next to the lock release lever instead of the pull knob at the window. Cabin door handles changed, doors now opened by squeezing the handle instead of using a push-button (change also applies to the crew-cab Pick-Up rear passenger door).
		Electric: due to changes in the primering procedure it was harder to make a ground connection with the bodywork through screws, so extra ground wires were added to the electrical system. Generator upgraded from 30A to 38A, voltage regulator changed accordingly. Symbol of oil warning light changed to the word 'Oil', Lamp now red instead of green. Interior light changed. Windscreen wipers now mounted with cap nuts (instead of clamped). Retaining spring for windscreen wiper blades changed.
		Other: tougher rear torsion bars introduced (became standard on Panelvan, Kombi without seats in back and Pick-Up models; other models kept more comfortable suspension).
	219 020 135	Connection of CV joints to gearbox changed. Clutch housing changed.
10.69		Odometer moved upwards on the speedometer dial from the lower half of the disc to the upper half. White hectometer counter with red letters added to the odometer ('tenth-mile' meter on vehicles with speedometer in miles).
	219 060 789	Inner rear-view mirror changed. Previously, standard was chrome, fitted to the ceiling with screws; now standard had a white vinyl surface, and was clamped with a spring.
	219 061 568	Switch for dual-circuit brake warning light (optional extra) now integrated with brake-light switches.
	219 098 975	Design of optional fresh-air ventilator changed.
	219 172 450	Screws for mounting turn signal switch on steering column changed.
	219 204 330	Different screw and matching screw cover used to fit dashboard plate between windscreen and dashboard.

1968 cabin door handle.

1969–79 cabin door handle.

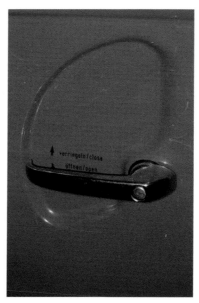
1968–73 sliding door handle.

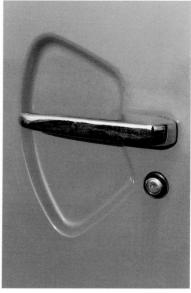
1974–79 sliding door handle.

Model year 1970
Chassis nos. 2102 000 001–2102 248 837

Month	Chassis no.	Change
08.69	2102 000 001	Start of model year 1970
		Engine: 30 PICT-3 carburettor replaces 30 PICT-2 carburettor (only on engines with M157).
		Front-axle steering: steering column tube attachment to dashboard changed. Front axle unit and distance between bolts for mounting it to the chassis enlarged.
		Chassis: diagonal beams added under cabin floor for more strength in case of an accident.
		Body and interior: dashboard no longer painted in body colour, now black; padded dashboards (M511) already in black only. Plastic dashboard rim given equal height over entire width, instead of having an upright rim at the steering wheel. Armrest of two-person middle bench seat changed. Handle for window winder now black for all vehicles (on Microbus Deluxe, old version with chrome arm still fitted). Lock-release lever bracket now made of black plastic instead of chrome (on Microbus Deluxe, chrome version still fitted). Inner rear-view mirror arm shortened. Sun visor shape changed to fit around the rear-view mirror.
		Electrics: warning buzzer for ignition key introduced (USA/Canada only), door contact switches introduced for operation of interior lights (for US market, left one also operates ignition-switch warning buzzer). Switches for horn and rotating light now united in a single knob. With new fuse box, relays can be plugged in rather than being connected with separate wires and mounted with a screw. Fuse box now holds twelve fuses instead of ten; has been relocated from under the dashboard rim to behind the fresh-air duct. Side marker reflectors become square-shaped (previously round), rear reflectors are equipped with a bulb (USA/Canada only). TL lamp changed and becomes available as optional extra (previously fitted only as standard equipment of Ambulance). Turn signal indicator lamp now has E-logo on it, lens in sideways direction changed (not for USA/Canada).
		Other: chrome wheel rims no longer fitted (previously standard on Microbus Deluxe).
09.69		Oil pipe with dome changed (engine no. B0 304 809)
	2102 106 748	VW starter motor is cancelled; Bosch starters only fitted from now on.

Model year 1971
Chassis nos. 2112 000 001–2112 300 000

Month	Chassis no.	Change
08.70	2112 000 001	Start of model year 1971
		Engine: 1600cc dual port engine with 50bhp, 34 PICT-3 carburettor and larger oil cooler. Valve for warm-air inlet on air filter operated by separate thermostat (previously with cable that connected to engine thermostat). Diaphragm clutch unit modified. Clutch release bearing changed.
		Front axle and steering: steering knuckle changed so disc brake calipers can be fitted.
		Wheels and brakes: disc brakes introduced on front wheels. Wheels changed: round ventilation holes added; mounting holes now closer to each other; wheels mounted with nuts (previously bolts); hubcaps flattened. Rear drum brake changed so new wheels can be fitted. Brake pads in rear drums changed to match drums.

Windscreen furniture

1968 wiper arm and jet.

1969–72 wiper arm and jet.

1973–79 wiper arm and jet.

Wheel arches

1968–70 wheel arch rear.

1971–79 wheel arch rear.

Body and interior: profile of rear wheel arches changed due to the use of different wheels. Keys and locks changed, keys are now 'profile R' (previously 'profile L'). Sliding-door mechanism changed. 'Drive only with sliding door locked' text on ignition switch housing now printed on silver sticker (previously painted in white letters). Rear crossmember below engine lid now mounted with two bolts instead of four.

Electrics: ignition lock now has three positions instead of four (garage position dropped). Headlamp switch swaps position on dashboard with interior light switch. Optional back-up lamp (M47) now 21W instead of 25W. Headlight relays made smaller to take less space in fuse box.

Month	Chassis no.	Change
15.12.70	2112 072 833	Speedo cable fitted with small plastic tube near steering damper to avoid damage through wear. Plastic band keeps cable in place to front axle body (RHD vehicles only).
	2112 102 250	Handle to operate flippable backrest on sliding door side(s) of middle bench changed.
01.01.71	2112 114 989	Camshaft changed (engine no. AD 136 656 and up)
	2112 138 001	Oil pump changed
	2112 168 837	Striker plate for luggage compartment hatch cancelled.
04.71		Second bleeder added to front brake caliper to make it possible to take more of the old brake fluid out when refreshing the system.
	2112 228 467	Test socket for electrical system introduced.

Front ends

1968–72 front.

1973–79 front.

Model year 1972
Chassis nos. 2122 000 001–2122 300 000

Month	Chassis no.	Change
08.71	2122 000 001	Start of model year 1972

Engine: Type 4 engine introduced as optional extra (1700cc). Type 1 engine: control box added to air filter. Metal accelerator cable guiding tube through fan housing changed. Beam that carries engine changed: previously two parts of sheet metal welded together, now one hollow beam bent into shape. Oil dipstick changed.

Fuel tank and heating: fuel tank changed, now with tank ventilation on engine air filter (was outside below tank opening). Two clamps introduced to hold fuel line above gearbox. Isolation of rear T-piece in hot-air tube changed. Optional fresh-air duct on cabin door changed. Optional air-circulation pipe for optional gas heater Eberspächer BN4 now made of one part instead of two.

Brakes: rear brake cylinder changed, brake shoes changed to match new brake cylinder.

Rear ends

1968–71 rear.

1972 rear.

1973–79 rear.

Chassis: transmission gets extra mounting point; now hangs on the chassis where it joins with the engine. Rear bumper and mounting changed; as a result, optional trailer hitch (M208) also changed. One crossmember added under rear side of cargo floor. Floor under fuel tank changed.

Body and interior: shape of lid for fuel filler opening changed, now with less round edges. Fuel filler cap made smaller, now with ribbed edge and without VW logo. Fuel filler opening moves backwards so that fuelling is possible with an open sliding door (all models except Pick-Up). Construction of rear end changed. Beam under engine lid now welded instead of bolted. Chassis number stamped on this beam from now on. Front wheel arch gets a profile round the edge. Ventilation opening introduced in cabin doors. Fresh-air inlets for the engine are enlarged, and made more square-shaped (previously more half-moon). Mud-protection plates between rear bumper edges and body cancelled. Luggage compartment hatch: finger grip shortened, hinges and locking mechanism changed. Engine hatch: locking mechanism changed, hatch smaller and different profiling above licence plate.

Electrics: big tail-lights replace small oval ones. Back-up lamps now integrated in the tail-light units; if a Bus has no option for these lights (M524, M603 or M616), there is no wiring connected. Connection 9 in diagnosis box now connected to no. 58 of left tail-light (was no. 58 of fuse box). To match various tyre sizes available, road-revolutions number on odometer changed (kms: old-0.5, new 0.51; miles: old-0.8, new 0.82). Dual-circuit brake warning lamp lights up when ignition is turned on, goes out when engine starts (previously light could be tested by pushing lens). Cable for starting motor changed. Ignition lock changed. Lens on knob of front foglamps now green (was black). Length of licence-plate light changed.

09.71		Cover for lower part of fan belt dropped (Type 1 engine).
	2122 069 752	Harness for stop-light switch and horn changed.
	2122 088 997	Relay for coupled headlamp flasher and licence-plate light cancelled (M30, for Austria only).
01.72		Battery protected from water by a cap on top (not for Pick-Up models).
	2122 228 467	Connection 17 in diagnosis box connected to mass-strip of battery.

Model year 1973
Chassis nos. 2132 000 001–2132 300 000

Month	Chassis no.	Change
08.72	2132 000 001	Start of model year 1973

Engine Type 1: crankcase ventilation now on air filter (was tube downwards from oil filler). Engine oil drain plate now without central drain plug.

Engine Type 4: inspection hatch in trunk introduced for vehicles with Type 4 engine (the ambulance, Type 27, remains without the inspection hatch). Paper-element air filter replaces oil-bath air filter (Type 4 engines without M157). Length of screw to mount hold strap around active carbon container shortened from 32 to 19mm (for vehicles with M157 only).

Fuel tank and heater: hot-air outlets under windscreen changed to start defogging in middle of windscreen rather than from the bottom. Wider and longer tube for heater outlet in between front-wheel wells (diameter 42 to 56mm, length 485 to 800mm). Hot-air distributor under cargo floor changed. Hot-air outlet moved from under rear bench seat to middle bench seat (only for Microbuses and Kombis with bench seats). Hose clamp for

Engine compartment

1968 without fire wall.

1968–79 fire wall.

Rotating light and siren switch

1970–79 rotating light and siren switch.

Air intakes

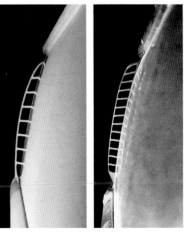

LEFT: T2a air-intake louvre (KN).
RIGHT: T2b air-intake louvre, prototype with twelve mouths instead of eight in the serial production (KN).

Seat adjustment

Adjuster knob for backrest (1968–73), handle for moving seat forward/backward (1968–76).

1974–79: handle for adjusting backrest.

1977–79: flat lever for moving seat forward/backward.

Volkswagen script

1968–72 Volkswagen script.

isolation of hot-air tube under rear of cargo floor changed. Rear T-piece of hot-air tube changed (previous version needed small profiling in rear of cargo floor). Diameter of hot-air tube under cargo floor increased from 69 to 100mm. Operation of hot-air distribution changed: left red handle now opens left and right heater box (previously left heater box), right red handle switches hot-air flow between either windscreen or cabin floor (previously opened right heater box, while handle under dashboard operated direction of air flow). Blue fresh-air handle now operates both fresh-air flaps under windscreen (previously two blue handles operated a flap each). Left hose of electrical fan in engine compartment made longer (from 450 to 640mm) (Type 4 engines). Right hose of electrical fan in engine compartment shortened (from 530 to 400mm) (Type 4 engines). **Transmission:** automatic transmission introduced as optional extra (M249).

Front axle and steering: worm and peg steering gear replaced by worm and roller steering gear.

Brakes: brake-fluid reservoir now mounted under driver's seat (previously under dashboard or behind driver's seat for vehicles with brake servo (M506)). Design of disc brakes and calipers changed, with bigger and stronger-built assembly.

Body and interior: VW logo diameter made smaller. Logo now mounted with three plastic clips. On all Bus models, logo of plastic in Pastel White L90D colour. Deluxe Microbuses and Buses with optional chrome trim (M521) get a plastic logo with chrome layer. 'Volkswagen' lettering cancelled from rear luggage compartment hatch. Square-shaped bumpers replace round-edged bumpers. Step for entering cabin now inside cabin instead of on bumper. Screws for fixing cover over sliding-door rails changed. Method of jamming sliding-door rails cover under side window changed. Seal between bodywork and sliding-door rails cover changed. Handle to operate flippable backrest on sliding door side(s) of middle bench changed. Roof opening of Westfalia pop-up roof (M518) moved forward 6cm (2.5in). Detachable headrest (M227) replaces headrest integrated in backrest (M258). Detachable headrest has zip to retain filling. On Pick-Up models the air for combustion now enters the car via the air vents on the right corner of the cabin. Chrome rim around front fresh-air inlet cancelled (was optional extra).

Electrics: front turn signals now fitted next to fresh-air inlet. The battery is turned 180 degrees to make battery poles more accessible. Windscreen wipers now operated with handles on steering column (was knob on dashboard), symbols added to handles on steering column. Windscreen wiper motor changed. Interval relay for windscreen wipers and wash/wipe function introduced as optional extra (M652). Windscreen washer jets and wiper arms now black instead of grey. Blue and red triangle mark and two symbols added beside fresh-/warm-air handles to indicate their operation. The triangles on the USA/Canada vehicles are illuminated and the symbols replaced with the words 'cold' and 'hot' to comply with regulations. Trip counter becomes available as optional extra (M25); fitted standard on Deluxe vehicles. Fuse box now fitted on fresh-air channel under dashboard to make it more accessible. Screws driven in clamps to hold instrument panel (previously driven into a frame welded in the dashboard). Warning lamp in hazard warning light switch burns with minimum strength. Can be regulated together with the brightness of the dashboard illumination (USA/Canada only). Word 'LIGHTS' added next to lamp symbol on headlamp switch (USA/Canada only). Ignition lock now has black plastic rim to prevent any reflections in the dashboard. Heavier sealed beam units applied. Low beam 40 to 50 watt, high beam 50 to 60 watt (only for vehicles with sealed beam units). Ground strap (transmission to chassis) changed. Front foglamps introduced as optional extra (M659) (previously available only on ambulances, and built in the bumper); French version has yellow lens. Relay of front foglamps changed. Lens on knob of front foglamps now yellow (was green). Rotating light: bulb replaced by halogen lamp (M160).

Other: tools supplied with vehicle now fitted in a bag together with the jack (previously in a tool roll, with separate jack). Retainer for jack under passenger seat no longer fitted.

1973: metal rim left and right of deformation element.

Month	Chassis no.	Change
	2132 006 265	Vehicles in the 2132 000 001–2132 006 265 range have four instead of six mounting points for trailer hitch bolts.
	2132 044 551	Gasket for gear carrier changed.
	2132 058 851	Diameter of hose between air filter and oil filler changed.
	2132 082 486	Connection 'V' of dual-circuit control lamp dropped.
	2132 082 848	Support for reverse lever in gearbox changed.
	2132 102 497	Ashtray on back of middle bench seat changed.
	2132 117 097	Alternator replaces generator (Type 1 engine).
01.02.73	2132 129 107	Clutch cable made 20mm longer.
	2132 138 901	Sender unit for fuel gauge changed.
	2132 166 508	'Vibrator' for fuel gauge introduced, making the gauge less sensitive to waves in the fuel tank, for a more reliable reading.
	2132 172 577	One rear crossmember under cargo floor removed.
	2132 174 859	Lock rings used for nuts to mount rear bench no longer fitted (crew-cab Pick-Up models).
	2132 174 859	Spring in cabin door window guide mounting cancelled.
	2132 178 701	Windscreen wiper blades changed.
	2132 194 782	Studs with nuts for mounting clutch-release bearing guide replaced by bolts.
	2132 226 539	Cylinder head changed (Type 1 engine).

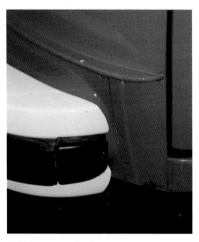

1974–79: connection between body parts flattened.

Model year 1974
Chassis nos. 2142 000 001–2142 300 000

Month	Chassis no.	Change
08.73	2142 000 001	Start of model year 1974

Engine Type 1: exhaust and damper pipe changed. Sealing ring for preheater pipe changed. Strengthened exhaust valves.

Engine Type 4: 1800cc engine replaces 1700cc in Buses equipped with Type 4 engine (all countries except USA and Canada).

Heater: optional gas heater changed: Eberspächer type BN4 (placed in engine compartment) replaced by type BA6 (placed under cargo floor in standard heater system). RHD vehicles with gas heater still get the BN4 type however.

Transmission: gearbox with ratios for 1800cc engine (Type 4 engines only). Selector handle of automatic gearbox now operated with knob on left side. Previously the handle had to be squeezed.

Body and interior: cabin floor changed. Fuel filler cap changed and no longer covered by a lid. Paint surface on metal dashboard now rough instead of smooth (vehicles without M511). Deluxe models now also get black window winder, as on regular models. Lock-release lever bracket for Microbus Deluxe (Type 24) now also made of black plastic instead of chrome, as on regular models. Sliding roof no longer standard on Microbus Deluxe. Locking the cabin door from the inside now done by pulling knob at window, as in first model year. Design of knob different however (change also applies to crew-cab Pick-Up rear passenger door). Sliding door handle changed. Lock now below handle instead of inside handle. Lock now also connected to the inside. Previously, locking

1968–72 handle for directing hot air to either the windshield or cabin floor.

Heater controls

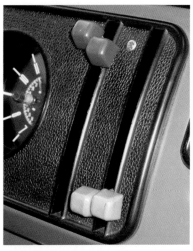

1968–72: two heater levers and two fresh-air levers.

1973–75: coloured symbols and single fresh-air levers.

1976–79: new symbols.

the door from the inside meant it could not be unlocked from the outside. Screw caps introduced for sliding door mechanism screws (only Type 22 and 27). Securing ring under screw that mounts inner sliding door handle cancelled. Roof opening of Westfalia pop-up increased in size (M73 replaces M518).

Electrics: meters on dashboard no longer have light grey dish with chrome rim in centre; now dark grey. Green parking light indicator lamp dropped. New headlamps (rims need to be taken off to adjust headlamps; previously, adjustment screws were in rims). Lens and reflector of optional front foglamps (M659) become separate parts. Relays for electrical fan in engine compartment changed (Type 4 engines). 'Top dead centre sensor' introduced.

Brakes: self-adjusting rear brakes introduced (Sweden only).

Month	Chassis no.	Change
08.10.73	2142 041 316	Selector fork for third/fourth gear changed to solve gear-shift problems with these gears.
01.11.73	2142 057 730	1800cc engine replaces the 1700cc in Buses equipped with Type 4 engine (USA and Canada).
	2142 079 204	Windscreen-wiper motor changed, screws for tail-light lens changed, harness for stop light switch and horn changed.
	2142 094 430	Crankcase of 1600cc engine is made of new 'AS 21' alloy.
	2142 110 465	Gearshift lever changed.
	2142 125 001	Bolts for mounting clutch unit to flywheel replaced by socket-head screws (Type 4 engine). Clutch disc size enlarged from 210 to 215mm (Type 4 engine).
	2142 132 408	Fuel injection introduced on Type 4 engines (USA-California only).
	2142 145 460	Windscreen-wiper motor changed.
	2142 145 593	Fuel filter in fuel tank changed.
	2142 158 936	Harness for stop light switch and horn changed.
	2142 164 060	Dashboard and steering column changed, leading to changes to following items: new, edge-shaped, design of turn signal and windscreen-wiper switches; steering wheel attachment to the steering column; ignition lock now facing upwards instead of being horizontally positioned; ignition lock cover made of plastic instead of metal; attachment of steering column to dashboard.
	2142 174 730	Reinforcement for side member, outer and crossmember of Pick-Up bed removed (Pick-Up models).
	2142 174 971	Studs with nuts in gearbox housing replaced by zinced bolts for better protection against contact-corrosion.
07.74		Outlet valve diameter narrowed from 32 to 30mm (Type1 engines, engine number AS 194 453).

Model year 1975
Chassis nos. 2152 000 001–2152 300 000

Month	Chassis no.	Change
08.74	2152 000 001	Start of model year 1975

Engine Type 1: paper element air filter replaces oil bath filter.
Engine Type 4: catalyst fitted on Buses for California, USA (M27), resulting in an 'Unleaded fuel only' sticker being fixed at the fuel filler opening and one on the windscreen. Screw and ring for mounting air-filter console changed (M6 screw becomes M8). Cylinder head changed: inlet valve 39.3 (was 41), outlet valve 32 (was 34). Electric parts of fuel-injection system changed. Fuel injection now fitted on Type 4 engines in all Buses for USA and Canada.
Heater: exhaust pipe of optional gas heater Eberspächer BA6 now ends on left side of vehicle (was under rear bumper).
Body and interior: engine-lid handle and rear-hatch handle changed from chromed to black plastic. Outer rear-view mirrors now made of steel and painted Pastel White L90D (stainless-steel version previously standard, but now delivered only on Deluxe

models and on Buses with the 'chrome' option (M181)). Backrest adjustment of driver's seat now done with handle on right side of seat instead of round knob under seat.

Electrics: interior light in cargo/passenger compartment no longer operated from dashboard, now has contact switch for the sliding door. Alternator changed (Type 4 engine). 70A alternator becomes available as option (M618) on Type 4 engines. Suppressor for ignition coil cancelled (only on suppressed versions). Division relay changed.

2152 017 116	Pull-back spring introduced to seat in ambulance compartment (Ambulance only). Aluminium stretcher changed (Ambulance only).
2152 030 081	Rear-window guide channel in cabin door cancelled
2152 049 803	Optional headrest changed to one solid unit (previously upholstery with filling, closed with zip).
2152 063 307	Hose clamp for isolation of hot-air tube under rear of cargo floor changed.
2152 064 869	Spring for headlamp bulb fitting changed. Sealing cap for headlamp bulb connection changed. Grommet for citylight changed (not for sealed beam).
2152 070 174	Sealing cap for halogen headlamp connection changed.
2152 073 084	Vacuum hose for brake servo now has textile surface for protection again dry-out cracks.
2152 088 258	Door contact switch for interior light now fitted without a seal.
2152 112 219	Bracket for windscreen-washer hose dropped.
2152 147 353	Fuel filter in fuel tank cancelled (from now on fuel filter is external).
2152 153 093	Lens and reflector of optional front foglamps (M659) become one single part. Central lock of sliding door changed (Type 21 only).
2152 153 713	Diameter of hinge pin in cabin door made smaller. Plastic plug to cover hinge-pin hole dropped.

Model year 1976
Chassis nos. 2162 000 001–2162 300 000

Month	Chassis no.	Change
08.75	2162 000 001	Start of model year 1976

Engine: bolts to mount engine to gearbox made longer, left bolt from 70 to 88mm, right bolt from 110 to 123mm (Type 1 and 4 engines).

Engine (Type 1): throttle valve damper added to 34-PICT-3 carburettor (1600cc engine). Stud for engine to gearbox mount made longer (from 82 to 97mm). Engine with special pistons introduced. Fan housing changed (only for Austria).

Engine (Type 4): optional Type 4 engine enlarged from 1800cc to 2000cc. Type 4 engine now also available for Pick-Up models (without inspection hatch in cargo floor). Air filter for dusty regions introduced. Clutch disc size enlarged from 215 to 228mm. Clutch-release bearing changed. Bolts for mounting clutch unit to flywheel are replaced by socket-head screws. Studs for mounting engine to gearbox made longer (from 85 to 97mm). Inlet valve valve 37.5 (was 39.3).

Heater: tube to heater outlet in between front wheel wells lengthened (from 800 to 880mm). Design of mounting clamp for hot-air operating cable under dashboard changed, now clamped to body instead of fitted with a screw. Spring added for improved operation of hot-air distributor under cargo floor. Isolation for heater tube under cabin floor cancelled. Bend-piece in hot-air tube under front of cabin floor changed. Hot-air tube under cabin floor now one piece instead of two.

Transmission: gearbox types changed, from '002' to '091' (Type 1 and Type 4 engines); automatic gearbox now also

Ignition locks

1968–69 ignition lock.

1970–74 ignition lock.

1974–79 ignition lock.

1968–69 fuse box under dashboard rim.

Chrome inner rear-view mirror (1968–69). Hot-air outlet on edge of dashboard under windshield (1968–72).

33

Sun visors (1968). Dashboard in body colour (1968–69). Plastic dashboard rim thicker in vicinity of steering wheel (1968–69). Odometer in lower half of speedo dial (1968–69).

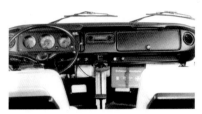

Anthracite odometer dial (1974–75), turn signal windshield wiper handles (1973–74).

Further details: *optional VW radio (Blaupunkt), trip recorder and clock (M25), dual circuit brake warning lamp (M50/M506), lockable glove compartment lid (M54), holder for first aid kit (M82), automatic gearbox diagram on ashtray (M249), padded surface on dashboard (M511), petrol heater knob left of ashtray (M60); right of ashtray: fog lamp switch (M571/M659) and rear window defroster (M102).*

1968–72 brake fluid container above kick-panel.

1972–73 fuel filler opening.

available on Pick-Up models (only with Type 4 engine). Operating cables and rods for automatic gearbox changed.

Chassis: rear crossmember under cargo floor changed. End crossmember for front side of cargo floor changed.

Electrics: meters on dashboard now have black background instead of grey. Instrument panel lights now white instead of green. 'EGR' and 'CAT' service interval indication lamps added to instrument panel (for USA and Canada only). Ground strap (transmission to chassis) changed (only on vehicles with automatic transmission). Starter motor changed (only on Buses with manual transmission). The handbrake control light is introduced as part of M50. Interior light is made smaller and more square-shaped. Cover on distributor cap for vehicles with suppression equipment changed. Spark-plug wires with cover over plug (only on suppressed versions).

Other: grommet for fuel hose changed (Type 4 engines with FI).

2162 016 734	Central mechanism of sliding door changed (Panelvan mechanism only).
2162 030 413	Sliding-door hinge and roller carrier on guide rail under rear side window changed.
2162 035 001	Screw that holds sliding door rails cover cancelled.
2162 047 257	Cabin doors: rail for ventilation slide now welded to door instead of riveted.
2162 067 001	Sweden introduced exhaust emission control (M62).
2162 077 584	Electronic control unit and wiring for fuel injection changed.
2162 090 464	Side marker reflectors get black rims (previously chrome); rear reflector screws changed (USA/Canada).
2162 100 001	Retaining spring for windscreen wiper blades changed.
2162 110 526	Small ring added for screws that mount sliding-door lock/latch to bodywork under rear side window.
2162 113 579	Seal for screw for tumbler-axe mounting dropped (Type 1 engine).
2162 118 505	Clutch disc size enlarged from 200 to 215mm (Type 1 engine).
2162 120 001	Holder for searchlight changed (Ambulance only).
2162 126 632	Hinges of cabin doors changed. Design changes involve different hinge mountings on body. Bolts now being used instead of socket-head screws.
2162 137 724	Bolts for mounting clutch unit to flywheel replaced by socket-head screws (Type 1 engines).
2162 143 427	Fan housing becomes the same as those on Austrian engines (Type 1 engines).

Model year 1977
Chassis nos. 2172 000 001–2172 153 964

Month	Chassis no.	Change
08.76	2172 300 000	Start of model year 1977

Engine Type 1: exhaust pipe now one piece without damper (previously out of a damper pipe with a bent end piece). Sealing ring between exhaust pipe and exhaust changed, previously needed a covering ring for solidity, now this ring is welded to the exhaust pipe.

Engine Type 4: hydraulic valve lifters introduced (only on GE engine). Electronic control unit for fuel injection changed.

Fuel tank: clamps for fuel line changed. Previously, fuel lines clicked into clamps, now clamps surround entire fuel line and then clamp into chassis.

Body: hinges of engine lid simplified, hinges of lid for access to compartment under cargo-floor compartment simplified (single-cab Pick-Ups only). Rails of driver's seat changed; change to handle that releases mechanism to allow seat to slide. Guide roller on bottom of sliding door changed.

Electrics: optional rear turn signal indicators on roof (M546) now round. Illumination on both front and rear.

2172 021 617	Exhaust emission control engine introduced (Sweden).
2172 053 839	Gearshift rod now with one bearing in rear instead of two.
2172 063 616	Special heater box introduced for Australia to match exhaust emission control system (Type 4 engine).
2172 078 763	Ground strap, stop tail-light right changed.
2172 100 001	Sealed beam holder changed.
2172 104 176	Bulb for searchlight changed (Ambulance only).
2172 137 043	Door check design changed.
2172 138 001	Fresh-air flaps under windscreen changed. Different hinges and foam seal used instead of rubber.
2172 145 277	Cover for 45A battery changed (cap not used on Pick-Up models).
2172 150 000	Grommet for opening of electrical wiring in tail-light units dropped.
2172 157 447	Construction of two-person passenger seat in cabin changed.

Model year 1978
Chassis nos. 2182 000 001–2182 153 964

Month	Chassis no.	Change
08.77	2182 000 001	Start of model year 1978

Engine: T-piece in tubes of tank ventilation changed, now made of plastic (was rubber). Active carbon container for absorbing fuel vapour moved from above engine to behind right tail-light (only for vehicles with exhaust emission control). Heater flap boxes each get an additional pipe for leading out hot air when this is not directed to interior (Type 4 engines with exhaust emission control).
Electrics: test socket for diagnosis system discontinued. Parking-light bulb fitted in headlamp unit with bayonet fitting (not for sealed beam). Dual-circuit brake warning lamp enlarged, now reads 'Brake' and 'Park brake' (Australia only).

Model year 1979
Chassis nos. 2192 000 001–2192 153 964

Month	Chassis no.	Change
08.78	2192 000 001	Start of model year 1979

Engine Type 4: catalyst now fitted on all engines for USA and Canada. Exhaust ports on cylinder heads now rectangular-shaped instead of circular, resulting in heater boxes being changed accordingly.
Electrics: 'OXR' light on instrument panel replaces 'CAT' service interval indicator lamp on vehicles for California, USA (M27).

05.79		Production of new Transporter (T3) starts while the Bay Window still rolls off the assembly line.
10.79	2192 153 964	Last Bay Window.

Dashboard

1968–69: lower-placed odometer, warning lamps without symbols.

1969–73: higher-placed odometer, warning lamps with symbols.

1974–75 speedo with anthracite background and new warning-lamp symbols.

1968–69 chassis without diagonal beams under cabin floor.

Safety improvements

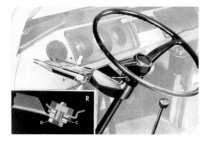

1970–74, improved safety: energy-absorbing steering-column support.

1970–79, improved safety: extra support beam in cabin doors.

1970–79, improved safety: extra diagonal beams under cabin floor.

THE CABIN DOOR

Locking Mechanism

1968 models were locked from the inside by lifting a pin placed near the window. In the period 1969–73 a small switch handle above the release lever replaced the pin. In 1974 the pin system was re-introduced, and the pin had a flat top.

Opening Mechanism

The release lever for opening the cabin door was chromed until the lock mechanism with the pin was introduced, in 1974. The bracket for the release lever was chromed during 1968–69. In 1970 it remained on the Microbus Deluxe but was replaced by a black plastic version on all the other models.

Pull Strap

The ends of the pull strap are fixed with screws to the cabin-door frame. The two points are covered with a plastic cap with a chrome layer. In model year 1970 this chromed version was replaced by an all-black one, except on the Microbus Deluxe. The Deluxe kept the chromed version until chassis number 2422 003 783 (1972).

Window Winder

In the first two years the window winder was chromed, with a black plastic cover over the handle and knob. In 1970 the plastic covered the entire window winder. The Microbus Deluxe kept the chrome version until it was replaced by the black version in 1974.

NOTE: All the above changes also apply to the rear passenger door of the crew-cab Pick-Up.

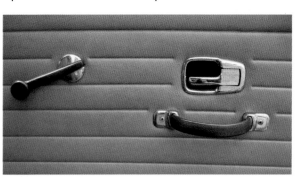

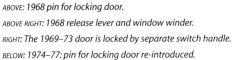

ABOVE: 1968 pin for locking door.
ABOVE RIGHT: 1968 release lever and window winder.
RIGHT: The 1969–73 door is locked by separate switch handle.
BELOW: 1974–77: pin for locking door re-introduced.

T1–T5: all generations in front of the Hannover client centre.

model and aggregate codes

Volkswagen models were divided into two distinct automotive lines – passenger cars and light commercial vehicles. The Beetle was referred to as 'Type 1', since it was the first car that Volkswagen took into volume production. It follows logically, therefore, that the Transporter, being the second type of vehicle in volume production, was called 'Type 2'. In this context, the term 'Type 2' refers to all generations of VW Transporters and Microbuses.

The five generations of VW Bus are represented by the following names: Type 2-T1 for the first generation of Transporters (Split Screen), T2 for the Bay Window, T3 for the Vanagon or Type 25, and T4 for the Eurovan. The most recent Transporter is called the T5.

The M-plate has a four-digit number for identifying the model and a two-digit code for the aggregate. The model code always starts with a '2', for 'VW Type 2'. The second number identifies the model. The third refers to the configuration – LHD or RHD. Specific model information is given by the fourth number, which refers to one or more optional extras.

The first number in the aggregate code represents the engine type fitted. The second digit gives the transmission type.

Interior of a Type 21 in standard configuration.

The tables here list all the model codes that were used. Different combinations were possible, so each table first shows all the variations in the first three numbers, then gives the optional variations.

BASIC SPECIFICATIONS BY MODEL

The basic configuration of each model is described below, and a customer could decide either to order optional extras or to leave certain items out in order to reduce costs. These modifications are described as M-codes (*see* Chapter 7).

Type 21 Panelvan

Two single passenger seats in the cabin and walk-through to cargo compart-

ment. The headliner is applied only to the cabin. The spare tyre is fitted on the left side above the engine. 1969–79: equipped with stronger torsion bars.

Cargo compartment: no windows in the side panels; no hardboard interior panels; no fresh- or hot-air outlet in the cargo compartment.

Type 22 Microbus and Microbus L

Fitted with softer rear torsion bars for more comfort, and chrome hubcaps. **Interior:** two single passenger seats in the cabin and walk-through to passenger compartment. Glove compartment lid. The spare tyre is fitted on the left side above the engine and has a plastic cover over it.

The passenger compartment is equipped with two three-seater benches. Interior panels with upholstery, coat hooks. The cabin doors have ventilation ducts on them to lead fresh air to the passenger compartment. Hot-air outlets are fixed to supply each bench seat in the rear. Headliner is applied all over the roof of the Bus and goes down to the interior panels.

1968–76: armrests fixed on trim panels in passenger compartment (except on sliding door).

1968–71: ventilation window in sliding door and opposite rear side panel (two ventilation windows altogether).

For Microbus Deluxe description, *see* Type 24.

Type 23 Kombi

Strong torsion bars for rear axle (except for Kombis of model year 1968, and the Kombis delivered with seats in the cargo compartment, they have the more comfortable Microbus torsion bars), one hot-air outlet for cargo compartment.

Interior: two single passenger seats in the cabin and walk-through to cargo compartment. No bench seats in the cargo compartment. The headliner is applied only to the cabin.

1968–71: ventilation window in sliding door and opposite rear side panel.

Type 24 Microbus L

The Type 24 is the same as the Type 22. In 1974 the model code 24 was dropped and the Deluxe Bus became a variation in the Type 22 coding. To see whether a Microbus is a Deluxe, the fourth digit in the model code must be deciphered (*see* table on page 39).

The Deluxe Bus had a number of interesting extras. In April 1968 the steel sliding roof was introduced on the Bay

Window (chassis no. 248 133 164 onwards). It became standard for the Deluxe until the start of model year 1974. The other standard extras were: clock in dashboard, ventilation windows in cabin doors, rubber strips on bumpers, guard rails behind rear window, on rear bench and rear side window on the right (also on the left if spare tyre is located in the cabin).

1973–79: trip counter in odometer.

No Deluxe vehicle is complete without a chrome set. The range of chromed parts includes the VW logo on the front and the strip around the windows.

1968–73: strips on belt line around the Bus.

1974–79: strips on rubber strip left and right side of Bus, fixed at the height of the cabin-door handles.

1968–72: rim around fresh-air inlet.

1968–69: trim rim in wheels.

Type 26 Pick-Up

SINGLE-CAB

One cargo lid for accessing cargo compartment under pick-up bed. Spare tyre is located under the bench seat in the cabin. Metal gates. 1969–79: tougher torsion bars for rear axle.

Interior: single seat for driver and two-person passenger seat in cabin.

CREW-CAB

One door for passenger compartment. Spare tyre located under the front bench seat in the cabin. Metal gates.

1969–79: tougher torsion bars for rear axle.

Interior: single seat for driver and two-person passenger seat in cabin. Three-person bench in rear. Fibreboard side panels in passenger compartment. One hot-air outlet for passenger compartment.

Type 27 Ambulance

Single seat for driver and two-person passenger seat in cabin. Dividing wall with sliding window. Spare tyre located under bench seat in cabin. Comfortable rear torsion bars, as on the Microbus. Chrome hubcaps. Illuminated roof sign with Red or Maltese Cross. Searchlight on inside of windscreen. Back-up lamps. Automatic step on sliding door.

Rear compartment: with ivory headliner down to trim panels. Ivory trim panels. Ventilation window in sliding door and opposite rear side panel. Lower half of rear windows is blinded, closets, stretcher seats, roof ventilator. Transistorized roof light in the rear, special hot-air outlet with adjustable jet and buzzer installation for patient to warn driver. For more details, *see* Chapter 11.

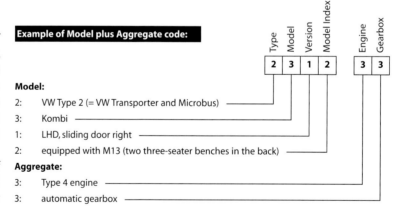

Example of Model plus Aggregate code:

| | | | | | | | | Type | Model | Version | Model Index | | Engine | Gearbox |

| 2 | 3 | 1 | 2 | | 3 | 3 |

Model:

2: VW Type 2 (= VW Transporter and Microbus)

3: Kombi

1: LHD, sliding door right

2: equipped with M13 (two three-seater benches in the back)

Aggregate:

3: Type 4 engine

3: automatic gearbox

Type 21.

Type 21-515.

Model codes

2 1 . . . .   **Panelvan**

Model code	Specifications	M-codes	Ch.plate	Years
2 1 1	LHD, sliding door right	–	–	all
2 1 4	RHD, sliding door left	–	–	all
2 1 5	LHD, two sliding doors	–	–	1968–73
2 1 6	RHD, two sliding doors	–	–	1968–73
. . . 0	Standard version	–	21	all
. . . 1	Fire Truck	M140	21 F	all
. . . 2	High-roof Panelvan	M516	21-515	all
. . . 3	High-roof Panelvan with high-roof sliding door	M515	21-515	all
. . . 9	Karmann Camper	M575	21	1978–79

Type 22.

2 2 . . . .   **Microbus and Microbus L**

Model code	Specifications	M-codes	Ch.plate	Years
2 2 1	LHD, sliding door right	–	–	all
2 2 4	RHD, sliding door left	–	–	all
2 2 5	LHD, sliding door right, sliding roof	–	–	1968–73
2 2 8	RHD, sliding door left, sliding roof	–	–	1968–73
. . . 0	Eight-seater, seat arrangement 2-3-3	–	22	all
. . . 1	Seven-seater, seat arrangement 2-2-3	M147	28	1968–73
	Eight-seater, seat arrangement 2-3-3 – Deluxe	M603	22	1974–79
. . . 2	Nine-seater, seat arrangement 3-3-3	M501	22	1968–73
	Eight-seater, seat arrangement 3-2-3	M147 500	22	1974–79
. . . 3	Eight-seater, seat arrangement 3-2-3 – Deluxe	M147 500 603	22	1974–79
. . . 4	Eight-seater, seat arrangement 3-2-3	M147 500	22	1968–73
	Nine-seater, seat arrangement 3-3-3	M501	22	1974–79
. . . 5	Nine-seater, seat arrangement 3-3-3	M500	22	1968–73
	Nine-seater, seat arrangement 3-3-3 – Deluxe	M501 603	22	1974–79
. . . 6	Nine-seater, seat arrangement 3-3-3	M500	22	1974–79
. . . 7	Nine-seater, seat arrangement 3-3-3 – Deluxe	M500 603	22	1974–79
. . . 8	Seven-seater, seat arrangement 2-2-3	M147	22/28	1974–79
. . . 9	Seven-seater, seat arrangement 2-2-3 – Deluxe	M147 603	28	1974–79

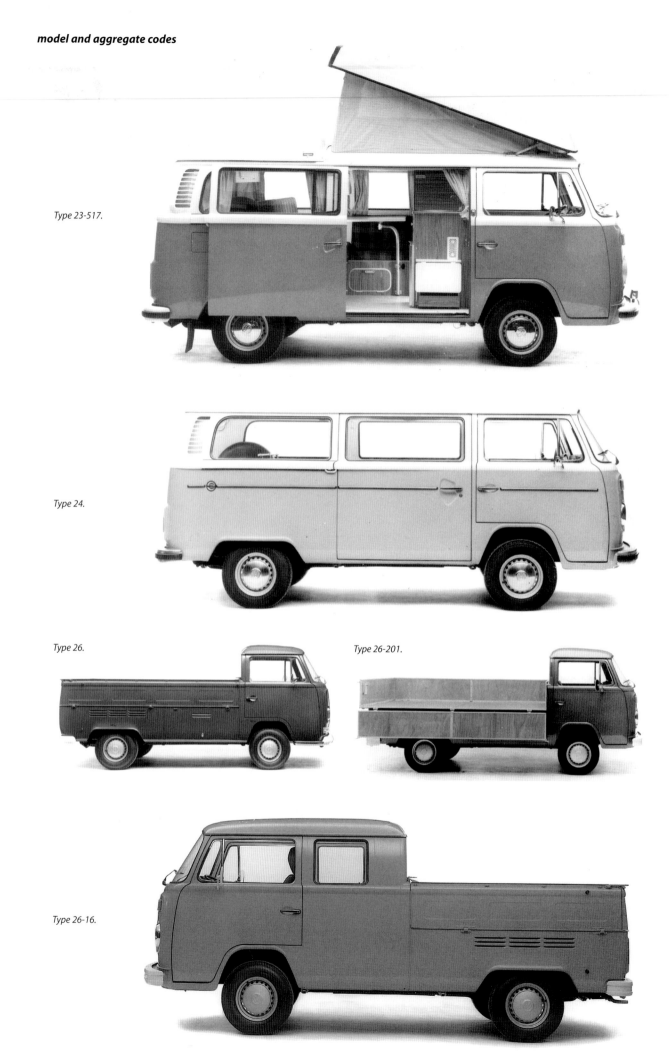

Type 23-517.

Type 24.

Type 26.

Type 26-201.

Type 26-16.

Model codes (*continued*)

2 3	**Kombi**			
Model code	**Specifications**	**M-codes**	**Ch.plate**	**Years**
2 3 1	LHD, sliding door right	–	–	all
2 3 4	RHD, sliding door left	–	–	all
2 3 5	LHD, sliding door right, sliding roof	–	–	1968–73
. . . 0	Standard version	–	23	all
. . . 1	Fire brigade vehicle	M140	23	all
. . . 2	Seat arrangement 2-3-3	M013	23	1972–79
. . . 3	Seat arrangement 2-3-0	M015	23	1972–79
. . . 4	Seat arrangement 2-2-3	M146	23	1972–79
. . . 6	Seat arrangement 2-0-3	M177	23	1972–79
. . . 9	Campmobile	M609	23-517	1972–79

2 4	**Microbus L**			
Model code	**Specifications**	**M-codes**	**Ch.plate**	**Years**
2 4 1	LHD, sliding door right	–	–	1968–73
2 4 4	RHD, sliding door left	–	–	1968–73
. . . 0	Eight-seater, seat arrangement 2-3-3	–	24	1968–73
. . . 1	Seven-seater, seat arrangement 2-2-3	M147	24	1968–73
. . . 4	Eight-seater, seat arrangement 3-2-3	M500	24	1968–73
. . . 5	Nine-seater, seat arrangement 3-3-3	M500	24	1968–73

2 6	**Pick-Up Single-Cab and Double-Cab**			
Model code	**Specifications**	**M-codes**	**Ch.plate**	**Years**
2 6 1	Single-cab, LHD, locker lid right	–	–	all
2 6 4	Single-cab, RHD, locker lid left	–	–	all
. . . 0	Standard version	–	26	all
. . . 1	Extended wooden platform	M201	26-201*	all
2 6 5	Double-cab, LHD, cabin door right	–	–	all
2 6 8	Double-cab, RHD, cabin door left	–	–	all
. . . 0	Standard version	–	26-16*	all

* from 1977 onwards: '26'.

Type 27.

27	Ambulance			
Model code	**Specifications**	**M-codes**	**Ch.plate**	**Years**
2 7 1	LHD, sliding door right	–	–	all
2 7 4	RHD, sliding door left	–	–	all
. . . 0	Standard version	–	27	all

. . . . . .	Aggregate			
Model code	**Specifications**	**M-codes**	**Ch.plate**	**Years**
. . . . 0	Type 4 engine – fuel injection	M062 157 608	–	1976–79
. . . . 1	Type 1 engine	–	–	all
. . . . 2	Type 1 engine – exhaust emission control	M157	–	1968–71
. . . . 3	Type 4 engine	M251	–	1972–79
. . . . 4	Type 4 engine – exhaust emission control	M157 251	–	1972–74
. . . . 5	Type 1 engine – stiff instead of torsion suspended clutch plate**	M126	–	
. . . . 6	Type 4 engine – fuel injection	M157 251	–	1974–79
. 1	Manual transmission, 4-speed	–	–	all
. 3	Automatic transmission, 3-speed***	M249	–	1973–79

** This specification exists only on single-cab Pick-Ups (model 261 and 264).

*** Automatic transmission was available only with Type 4 engine.

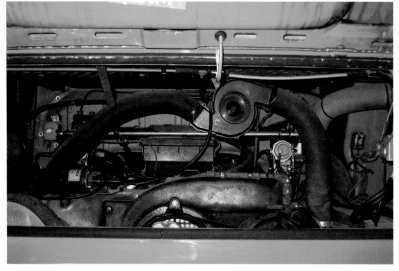

ABOVE LEFT: Type 1 engine.

ABOVE: Automatic transmission.

LEFT: Type 4 engine.

ENGINE TYPES AND DEVELOPMENT

In the first four years of the Bay Window there was very little variation in the engines. All the available engines in that period were so-called 'upright' or 'Type 1' engines, in reference to the car in which the engine was first put to use – the VW Beetle. The T2 got the strongest version of this, which had 1600cc and 47hp. For the North American market a modified engine was used to meet exhaust gas regulations (M157). California regulations required an additional activated carbon container for absorbing fuel vapours from the tank (M26).

Buses delivered to countries with a lower fuel quality got an engine with recessed crown pistons (M240). This modification made the engine a little less powerful, producing 44hp.

In August 1970, the upright engine was upgraded. A larger carburettor was fitted and the heads got a separate inlet for each cylinder. As a result, these engines are also called 'double-port engines'. (Logically, its predecessor is also known as 'single-port'.) The oil cooler was enlarged and placed outside the fan housing.

In January 1971 (M252) Italian Buses could be delivered with the less powerful 1300cc engine.

With the start of model year 1972, the design of the engine compartment was changed radically. The rear beam under the engine hatch was now welded to the chassis instead of bolted, making it harder to get the engine out of car. The engine's 'playground' had

been enlarged so the wider Type 4 engine could be fitted as optional extra M251. This 1700cc engine producing 66hp owes its name to the first Volkswagen that it propelled – the VW 411 ('VW Type 4'). The Type 4 engine had two carburettors, and the fan housing was placed against the rear of the car. This gave the engine a flat look, hence its nickname of 'pancake engine'. In the United States and Canada the Type 4 engine became standard equipment from the day it was first available (it was also equipped with the exhaust-gas recirculation device that was required to meet emission regulations). From 1973 on, the activated carbon container required for California became standard for the entire USA and Canada.

A special hatch was placed in the luggage compartment to give better access to the Type 4 engine. This hatch existed from model year 1973 onwards, but the Ambulance had to do without it.

In September 1973, the Type 4 engine was upgraded to 1800cc, producing 68hp. By the end of model year 1974 it had become more difficult to meet Californian regulations so an 1800cc engine with L-Jetronic fuel injection became available for this state. In August 1974 the fuel-injected engine became standard for the entire USA and Canada.

In August 1975 the pancake engine got its third and last 'cc' upgrade, when the 2000cc version replaced the 1800cc. The Type 4 engine was now also available in the Pick-Up models.

One fuel-injected version of the pancake engine was equipped with hydraulic valve lifters in August 1977.

This innovation meant that it was no longer necessary to adjust the valves, normally a frequent maintenance detail that was important in keeping a VW boxer engine alive.

The successor of the Bay Window, the Vanagon, was sold with both the Type 1 and Type 4 engine in the first years of production. The Type 1 engine was made flat in the same way as the Type 4 engine, by moving the fan housing to the rear of the car. In 1983 the Vanagon was no longer available as an air-cooled vehicle and this also meant the end of the pancake engine. The upright Type 1 engine, however, is still in production today, as the power source of the Brazilian T2.

Engine Survey

The table below shows all the engine variations that were fitted in the Bay Window. The engine numbers are given at three particular dates: at the beginning of each model year, on the last day of the calendar year, and on the last day of the model year. This should give owners a good chance of working out whether the engine of a particular Bus is still the original one.

The first column of the table shows the engine code as it appears in the aggregate code. The second column indicates whether it is an upright Type 1 or the flat Type 4 engine. The next columns show the engine size and power. Sometimes the engine number on the case is followed by an 'X' and the VW logo with arrows in a circle around it. Such engines have been revised by Volkswagen.

Engine numbers

Model year 1968

Engine code	Engine	cc	kW	bhp	M-code	01.08.1967 218 000 001	31.12.1967 218 073 585	31.07.1968 218 202 251
1	Type 1	1600	37	50	–	B0 000 001	B0 051 498	B0 137 105
		1600	32	44	M240	C0 000 001	C0 005 418	C0 017 008
2		1600	35	47	M157	B5 000 001	B5 017 663	B5 050 173

Model year 1969

Engine code	Engine	cc	kW	bhp	M-code	01.08.1968 219 000 001	31.12.1968 219 098 974	31.07.1969 219 300 000
1	Type 1	1600	37	50	–	B0 137 106	B0 198 647	B0 286 760
		1600	32	44	M240	C0 017 009	C0 025 903	C0 041 675
2		1600	35	47	M157	B5 050 174	B5 079 928	B5 116 436

(continued overleaf)

Engine numbers (*continued*)

Model year 1970

Engine code	Engine	cc	kW	bhp	M-code	01.08.1969 2102 000 001	31.12.1969 2102 106 747	31.07.1970 2102 248 837
1	Type 1	1600	37	50	–	B0 286 761	B0 361 088	B0 520 000
		1600	32	44	M240	C0 041 676	C0 047 984	C0 100 000
2		1600	35	47	M157	B5 116 437	B5 144 597	B5 230 000

Model year 1971

Engine code	Engine	cc	kW	bhp	M-code	01.08.1970 2112 000 001	01.01.1971 2112 114 989	31.07.1971 2112 300 000
1	Type 1	1300	32	44	M252	–	AB 142 001	AB 350 000
		1600	37	50	–	AD 000 001	AD 136 656	AD 350 045
		1600	34	46	M240	AF 000 001	AF 007 863	AF 016 002
2		1600	37	50	M157	AE 000 001	AE 155 611	AE 529 815

Model year 1972

Engine code	Engine	cc	kW	bhp	M-code	01.08.1971 2122 000 001	31.12.1971 2122 088 996	31.07.1972 2122 300 000
1	Type 1	1300	32	44	M252	AB 350 001	AB 384 573	AB 699 002
		1600	37	50	–	AD 350 046	AD 402 022	AD 612 163
		1600	34	46	M240	AF 016 003	AF 020 666	AF 031 621
3	Type 4	1700	49	66	M251	CA 000 001	CA 005 040	CA 017 215
4		1700	49	66	M157, 251	CB 000 001	CB 025 065	CB 060 640

Model year 1973

Engine code	Engine	cc	kW	bhp	M-code	01.08.1972 2132 000 001	31.12.1972 2132 102 496	31.07.1973 2132 300 000
1	Type 1	1300	32	44	M252	AB 699 003	AB 768 324	AB 990 000
		1600	37	50	–	AD 613 001	AD 739 408	AD 990 000
		1600	34	46	M240	AF 032 101	AF 040 284	AF 052 120
3	Type 4	1700	49	66	M251	CA 020 001	CA 029 721	CA 050 000
		1700	46	62	M249, 251	CE 000 001	CE 001 503	CE 004 500
4		1700	49	66	M157, 251	CB 062 001	CB 082 876	CB 101 138
		1700	46	62	M157, 249, 251	CD 000 001	CD 000 224	CD 008 722

Model year 1974

Engine code	Engine	cc	kW	bhp	M-code	01.08.1973 2142 000 001	31.12.1973 2142 094 429	31.07.1974 2142 300 000
1	Type 1	1300	32	44	M252	AR 000 001	AR 008 603	AR 009 252
		1600	37	50	–	AS 000 001	AS 117 378	AS 195 425
		1600	34	46	M240	AF 052 121	AF 090 783	AF 124 918
3	Type 4	1800	49	66	M251	AP 000 001	AP 011 746	AP 027 465
4		1700	49	66	M157, 251	CB 101 139	CB 110 000*	–
		1700	46	62	M157, 249, 251	CD 008 723	CD 011 000*	–
		1800	50	68	M157, 251	AW 000 001**	AW 018 536	AW 037 000
		1800	51	70	M27, 157, 251	–	ED 000 001***	ED 000 639

* Last engine 30.10.1973 (chassis no. 2142 057 729)

** Engine introduced 01.11.1973 (chassis no. 2142 057 730)

*** Fuel injection introduced March 1974 (chassis no. 2142 132 408)

Model year 1975

Engine code	Engine	cc	kW	bhp	M-code	01.08.1974 2152 000 001	31.12.1974 2152 073 083	31.07.1975 2152 300 000
1	Type 1	1300	32	44	M252	AR 009 253	AR 009 539	AR 010 000
		1600	37	50	–	AS 195 426	AS 251 574	AS 313 827
		1600	34	46	M240	AF 124 919	AF 190 624	AF 199 864
3	Type 4	1800	50	68	M251	AP 027 466	AP 037 047	AP 055 000
6		1800	50	68	M157, 251	ED 000 640	ED 011 950	ED 025 000

Model year 1976

Engine code	Engine	cc	kW	bhp	M-code	01.08.1975 2162 000 001	31.12.1975 2162 077 675	31.07.1976 2162 300 000
1	Type 1	1600	37	50	–	AS 313 828	AS 363 700	AS 426 296
		1600	34	46	M240	AF 199 865	AF 277 251	AF 349 315
3	Type 4	2000	51	70	M251	CJ 000 001	CJ 013 231	CJ 030 646
6		2000	51	70	M157, 251	GD 000 001	GD 010 983	GD 027 786
0		2000	51	70	M157, 251 (and 62 or 608)	–	GD 010 983	GD 027 786

Model year 1977

Engine code	Engine	cc	kW	bhp	M-code	01.08.1976 2172 000 001	31.12.1976 2172 081 316	31.07.1977 2172 300 000
1	Type 1	1600	37	50	–	AS 426 297	AS 477 889	AS 524 575
		1600	34	46	M240	AF 349 316	AF 408 636	AF 420 000
3	Type 4	2000	51	70	M251	CJ 030 647	CJ 041 410	CJ 054 702
6		2000	51	70	M157, 251	GD 027 787	GD 038 614	GD 055 800
0		2000	51	70	M157, 251 (and 62 or 608)	GE 000 001	GE 002 336	GE 007 082

Model year 1978

Engine code	Engine	cc	kW	bhp	M-code	01.08.1977 2182 000 001	31.12.1977 2182 072 273	31.07.1978 2182 300 000
1	Type 1	1600	37	50	–	AS 524 576	AS 563 435	AS 611 029
		1600	34	46	M240	AF 420 001	AF 478 279	AF 530 872
3	Type 4	2000	51	70	M251	CJ 054 703	CJ 065 563	CJ 081 816
6		2000	51	70	M157, 251	GE 007 083	GE 019 988	GE 039 331
0		2000	51	70	M157, 251 (and 62 or 608)	GE 007 083	GE 019 988	GE 039 331

Model year 1979

Engine code	Engine	cc	kW	bhp	M-code	01.08.1978 2192 000 001	31.12.1978 2192 073 637	31.07.1979 2192 153 964
1	Type 1	1600	37	50	–	AS 611 030	AS 644 291	AS 692 077
		1600	34	46	M240	AF 530 873	AF 538 084	AF 545 517
3	Type 4	2000	51	70	M251	CJ 081 817	CJ 094 385	CJ 110 966
6		2000	51	70	M62, 157, 251	GE 039 332	GE 049 407	GE 058 786
0		2000	51	70	M157, 251 (and 62 or 608)	GE 039 332	GE 049 407	GE 058 786

M-CODES USED (For full descriptions, *see* Chapter 7.)

M027 = Complies with California emission regulations	M157 = Fuel injection (1975–79)	M252 = 1300cc instead of 1600cc
M062 = Complies with Sweden emission regulations	M240 = Engine for low-octane fuel	M251 = Type 4 engine
M157 = Exhaust-emission standards (1968–74)	M249 = Automatic transmission	M608 = Complies with Australia emission regulations

GEARBOX SURVEY

The gearbox type is indicated by two letters, stamped on the left edge of the bottom of the transmission case. The two letters are followed by a serial number. No data can be found in Volkswagen literature about the meaning of the serial number on early Buses. Since 1 October 1972 (chassis no. 2132 036 148) the code represents the production date, with two numbers for the day, two numbers for the month and one number to indicate the year. For example, CP 28 03 8 would indicate a manual gearbox for a 2000cc engine, which was produced on 28 March 1978.

Gearbox types

4-speed manual transmission

Model code	Code	Engine	M-code	Gear ratios						Years
				1st	2nd	3rd	4th	Rev.	Final drive	
1	CA	1600		3.80	2.06	1.26	0.82	3.61	5.375	1968–71
	CB	1600	M92	3.80	2.06	1.26	0.82	3.61	5.857	1968–71
	CC	1600	M220	3.80	2.06	1.26	0.82	3.61	5.375	1968–71
	CD	1600	M092 220	3.80	2.06	1.26	0.82	3.61	5.857	1968–71
	CE	1600		3.80	2.06	1.26	0.82	3.80	5.428	1972–75
	CF	1600	M92	3.80	2.06	1.26	0.82	3.80	5.857	1972–75
	CG	1600	M220	3.80	2.06	1.26	0.82	3.80	5.375	1972–75
	CH	1600	M092 220	3.80	2.06	1.26	0.82	3.80	5.857	1972–75
	CK	1700	M251	3.80	2.06	1.26	0.82	3.80	5.375	1972–73
	CL	1700	M220 251	3.80	2.06	1.26	0.82	3.80	5.375	1972–73
	CM	1800	M251	3.80	2.06	1.26	0.89	3.80	4.857	1974–75
	CN	1800	M220 251	3.80	2.06	1.26	0.89	3.80	4.857	1974–75
	CP	2000	M251	3.78	2.06	1.26	0.88	3.28	4.571	1976–79
	CT	2000	M220 251	3.78	2.06	1.26	0.88	3.28	4.571	1976–79
	CU	1600		3.78	2.06	1.26	0.82	3.28	5.428	1976–79
	CV	1600	M220	3.78	2.06	1.26	0.82	3.28	5.428	1976–79
	CW	1600	M092	3.78	2.06	1.26	0.82	3.28	5.857	1976–79
	CX	1600	M092 220	3.78	2.06	1.26	0.82	3.28	5.857	1976–79

3-speed automatic transmission

Model code	Code	Engine	M-code	Gear ratios					Years
				1st	2nd	3rd	Rev.	Final drive	
3	NA*	1700	M249 251	2.65	1.59	1	1.80	4.45	1972–73
	NB	1700/1800	M249 251	2.65	1.59	1	1.80	4.36	1972–75
	NC**	1800	M027 157 249 251	2.65	1.59	1	1.80	4.36	1974
	ND	1800	M157 249 251	2.65	1.59	1	1.80	4.36	1975
	NE	2000	M249 251	2.55	1.45	1	2.46	4.10	1976–79
	NF	2000	M157 249 251	2.55	1.45	1	2.46	4.10	1976–79

*   The 'NA' gearbox was used until 30.10.1973 (until chassis no. 2142 057 729) on
     North American vehicles due to the delayed introduction of the 1800cc engine.

** Special version for California fuel injection engine, introduced 18.03.1974 (chassis no. 2142 132 408)

M-CODES USED (For full descriptions, *see* Chapter 7.)

M027 = Engine complies with California emission regulations

M092 = Mountain ratio

M157 = Engine with exhaust-emission control (1975 onwards: fuel injection)

M220 = Limited slip differential

M249 = Automatic transmission

M251 = Type 4 engine

M520.

optional equipment

M-CODES

Factory-fitted options are identified by their 'M' number or 'M-code', the 'M' standing for *Mehr- und Minderausstattung*, German for 'extra and reduced equipment'. Not all M-codes indicate an optional extra. Some describe equipment that was left out of the Bus, perhaps for legal reasons or because the buyer wanted to cut costs.

M560.

The M-code indicates the way in which a particular Bus differs from a defined standard version. For example, a basic Type 24 is a Deluxe Bus with a sliding roof as standard. If a customer did not want to have this specification, it was possible to order the Type 24 with M130, in other words '*without* steel sliding roof' (reducing the equipment). A regular Microbus (Type 22), on the other hand, did not come with a sliding roof as

standard. If a customer particularly wanted to have this specification, he could order under M-code M560 ('steel sliding roof'), thereby adding extra equipment.

This chapter lists four types of codes. They are all printed on the M-plate in the space where the M-codes are featured (*see* Chapter 3). The first list shows the M-codes M001–M699 and M800–M999, the second, S-codes S700–S799, the next, the special conversion codes, and the last, the group codes.

Certain optional equipment became standard or obsolete through the years, so M-codes were cancelled, and the cancelled codes were often re-used for a completely different item. To interpret such a code correctly, it is necessary to know the model years, and these are also indicated in the table. In some cases, chassis numbers were given to define the exact period of use for an M-code. Volkswagen used the chassis numbers of the Type 21 (the Panelvan) as a default in their documentation. These can easily be converted simply by replacing the '21' with type codes of other T2 models (*see* Chapter 6).

Optional equipment (M-codes)

M-code	Description	Model type	Yrs/prd	Remarks
002	With US-specific sealed beam headlamps, for M027: with US-specific carriers for catalysts (only with M524)	21, 22, 23 (LHD)		
005	Heater outlet in seat box of rear bench seat	231, 234		Westfalia Campmobiles
007	Without tyres	All		
008	Without battery	All		
010	Additional dust sealing for engine compartment	All	1968–73	To chassis no. 2132 102 496
012	Exhaust emission control installation and speedometer in miles instead of km (with M524 only)	21, 22, 23 (LHD)	1975–79	
013	Middle three-person bench seat, rear three-person bench seat and interior trim in passenger compartment	23		
015	Middle three-person bench seat and interior trim in passenger compartment	23		
018	With hazard light installation	21–26	1968	Sweden
019	Without headlamp flasher	All	1968–69	
020	Speedometer and odometer in miles	All		
024	Sealed beam headlamps	21–26	1968–69	Export, not Canada and USA
"	Sealed beam headlamps, side marker reflectors and reversing lights	21–26	1970–79	Export, not Canada and USA
025	Speedometer with trip recorder and clock	All	1973–79	
026	With activated carbon container for absorbing fuel vapour	All	1968–72	USA-California
"		21–23	1968–76	Japan
"		21–23	1976–79	Australia
027	Plate with emissions value and engine that complies to the California exhaust emission standards	21–23 (LHD)	1973–74	USA-California
"	Plate with emissions value, engine with catalyst	21–23 (LHD)	1975–79	USA-California
028	Without stretchers, also in combination with M152 (ambulance)	27	1970–79	
029	Towing hook front and rear	21–26	1968–71	
030	Coupled headlamp flasher and licence plate light	LHD		To chassis no. 2122 088 996, Austria
031	Battery approved by research and development department and free from import duty and costs	All		
032	Lockable cap for fuel tank	All		
033	Red Crescent lamp instead of Red Cross lamp	27		
034	Side turn signals, altered handbrake handle, white front turn signal lenses	LHD	1968–74	Italy

M25.

M32 – 1974–79.

M29 – rear.

M29 – front.

M-code	Description	Model type	Yrs/prd	Remarks
034	Side-mounted turn signals, altered handbrake handle, white front turn signals, without emergency light system, without hazard light system (France and Italy only)	LHD	1975–79	Italy
037	Without hazard light system	LHD	1968–74	Italy
042	Tyres approved by research and development department and free from import duty and costs	All		
046	Side turn signals and inner rear-view mirror	LHD	1969	
"	Side turn signals	LHD	1970–79	
047	Two reversing lights	21–26	1968–71	
050	Dual-circuit control light (only with M511)	All	1968–75	
"	Dual-circuit and handbrake control light	All	1976–79	
051	With pedestal and double pulley for the later installation of a second generator (not in combination with M153, M157 and M251)	All		
053	Cloth upholstery instead of leatherette	22, 24	1968–75	
054	Lockable glove compartment lid (only with M511)	All	1972–79	
055	With steering lock	All	1969	
056	With steering lock	All	1968	
057	Hardwood strips for flatbed not fastened to vehicle	261–268		
060	Eberspächer BA6 petrol heater (LHD) (fitted under cargo floor)	211–271	1974–79	
061	Type labelling of seat mounting and identification plate for England and Ireland	All		
062	Convex rear-view mirror, outer, right. Inner rear-view mirror with shorter arm	LHD	1968–69	Sweden
"	Sun visor, right without mirror	221–225, 241	1971–73	Sweden
"	Compliance with Sweden exhaust emission standards	21–26	1974–79	Sweden
064	Without sidegates and tailgate	26	All	
065	Writings for maximum axle loads and maximum weight	21, 26	All	
066	Floor cover (rubber mat) in passenger compartment	23		
067	12V 54A battery instead of standard 12V 45A battery	All		
068	Two front towing hooks	All	1972–79	
070	Tilt and bows for Pick-Up	261, 264		

M46.

M47.

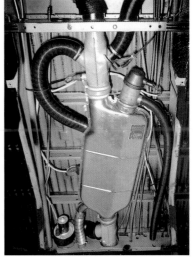

ABOVE RIGHT: *M51.*

RIGHT: *M60 – Gas heater under cargo floor. On the top of the picture is the beginning of the cabin floor. The black hose on the top left goes to the warm-air outlet under the middle bench.*

LEFT: *M70.*

Optional equipment (M-codes) (*continued*)

M-code	Description	Model type	Yrs/prd	Remarks
071	Second lid for underfloor cargo compartment	261, 264		
072	Battery under customs seal	All		
073	Roof opening and reinforcement for Westfalia pop-up roof SO 73	231, 234	1974–79	
074	Mud flaps, rear	21–26		
082	Mountings for first aid kit	LHD		
083	With warning triangle	All		
085	Filled in factory with double amount of petrol (used for driving on and off the train, for example)	All		
086	Self-adjusting drum brakes (rear)	All	1974–79	Sweden
089	Laminated windscreen glass	21–26	1969–79	
090	Laminated windscreen glass		1968	
092	Gearbox with mountain ratio for mountainous areas	All		
093	Ventilation windows in windows opposite sliding door	23		
094	Lockable engine lid	All	All	
095	Wolfsburg car radio	All		
096	Braunschweig car radio	All		
097	Emden car radio	All	All	
098	Ingolstadt car radio	All		
099	Tubeless off-road tyres	All		
100	Without VW logo on front	All		
101	Off-road tyres	All		
102	Rear-window heating	21–26	All	
106	Upholstery material, special version (cloth)	21–26		German Mail and Police
109	Removable prints 'Deutsche Bundespost' and 'Posthorn' logo	21–26		German Mail
111	Removable prints 'Deutsche Bundesbahn' and tyre-pressure text	21–26		
112	Removable prints 'Unicef'	All		
113	Admittance plate for Canada	21–23 (LHD)		
115	Prepared for low-loader Pick-Up	261, 264		
116	Surveyor measuring group vehicle. Same as M541 but with swivelling seat and table on division wall instead of bench (with M541 only)	231		German Mail
117	Without seats in rear	265, 268		
118	Altered heater outlet of optional petrol heater (only with M119)	211, 231	1973	
"	Duty-free tyres (duty refund)	All	1975–79	
119	Eberspächer BN4 petrol heater with outlet in load/passenger compartment	21–24	1968–72	
"	Eberspächer BN4 petrol heater with air recirculation connection and outlet in load/passenger compartment	21–24, 27	1973	
"	Eberspächer BN4 heater	21, 22, 23 (RHD)	1974–79	
120	Without mountings for seats and safety belts in cargo compartment	23	All	
121	Two electric ventilators in fresh-air system	All	All	
123	Suppression equipment for radio reception	All	All	

ABOVE: M82.

RIGHT: M119 with M514.

M-code	Description	Model type	Yrs/prd	Remarks
124	Yellow headlamp bulbs and safety inner rear-view mirror	All	1968–75	France
"	Yellow headlamp bulbs	All	1976–79	France
126	1600cc engine with stiff instead of torsion-suspended clutch disc	261, 264		
127	Rear panel lid without window	21–23, 27	All	
128	Whitewall tyres		1968–71	
130	Without steel sliding roof	24	1968–73	
131	Removable prints 'Deutsche Bundespost', 'Fernmeldedienst' and post horn logo	21-23, 261, 265		German Mail (telecommunications department)
133	Chassis plate without prints of the maximum total mass and the maximum axle loads	21–26		Israel, Switzerland, Thailand
134	Fold-down passenger seat	23		
140	Modifications for fire truck, front bumper mounted higher for taking steep slope; with laminated windscreen	21, 23	1968–72	
"	Modifications for fire truck, without deformation element behind front bumper; with laminated windscreen	21, 23	1973–79	
141	Heater outlet in rear part of cargo compartment		1968–72	
"	With heater outlet under middle bench seat	22, 23	1973–79	
145	With safety lock for sliding door(s) and rear panel lid	211, 215		
146	Middle bench seat (two persons), rear bench seat and interior trim in passenger compartment	231, 235		
147	Seven-seater model instead of eight-seater model	221, 225, 241	1968–73	
"	Seven-seater model instead of eight-seater model	221	1974–79	
148	With hinged rear seat backrest	221, 224	1974–76	
"	With hinged rear seat backrest	231, 234	1974–79	
149	Painted instead of chrome parts	All		
150	VW Ambulance according to requirement DIN 75080: two foglamps on bumper, protection plates for bottom, maximum tyre inflation written above the wheels, symbol notification of knobs on windscreen, reinforcement under upholstery for mounting of fire extinguishers in cabin, additional mountings for several pieces of equipment according to DIN requirement, transparent battery cases (only with M623)	271	All	
151	Eberspächer BN4 heater	27	1968–73	
"	Eberspächer BN4 heater	274	1974–79	
152	Simplified rails, plus stretcher on right-hand side	27		
153	Paper element cyclone air filter without carburettor pre-heating (1300 and 1600cc engines only)	All	1975–79	
155	Two oil bath air filters with larger oil capacity	All	1968–74	
156	Oil bath air filter with larger oil capacity for dusty regions	All	1968–74	
157	Exhaust emission control system	All	1968–71	
"	Exhaust emission control system and activated carbon container for absorbing fuel vapour	211, 221, 231	1972–75	
"	Fuel injection engine	211, 221, 231	1975–79	

M127.

M145 on sliding door.

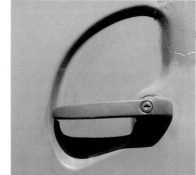

M149.

Optional equipment (M-codes) (*continued*)

M-code	Description	Model type	Yrs/prd	Remarks
159	Securing plate and rings for padlock	211, 231	1975–79	German Mail
160	Blue rotating light and siren	All	All	
161	Seats in cabin with mountings for headrests	all	1973–79	
162	Rubber strips for bumpers	All	1973–79	
168	Gauged trip writer	All		
171	Tubeless textile or steel-ply tyres	21–26		
172	Tubeless steel-ply tyres	All		
176	C-shaped guiding rails on metal partition between cabin and cargo compartment and on the side opposite the sliding door (for model 211 only with M540, for model 231 only with M120, M540)	211, 231		
177	Three-seater bench in the back and interior trim	231		
178	Wooden floor panels with built-in guiding rails (also in side panels and on floor above engine compartment) for mounting tools and instruments	231		
180	Without three-seater middle bench seat	22, 24		
181	Chrome hubcaps	21, 23, 26, 27	1968–72	
"	Chrome hubcaps and headlamp rings	21, 23, 27	1973–74	
"	Chrome hubcaps, headlamp rings and rear-view mirror	21, 23, 27	1975–79	
182	With seatbelt mounting points for folding seat in rear compartment	271	1973	Austria
184	Three-point safety belts for driver and passenger seat with roll-up automatic and push-button lock	All		
185	Seatbelts for all factory-mounted seats in cabin and in passenger compartment	211–244	1972–79	USA and Canada
186	Two-point seatbelts for all seats in passenger compartment	All		
187	Headlamps for countries with left-hand traffic	All		
188	Simplified heating system with special heater boxes, no isolation on hot-air ducting, no noise isolation on front of car and on front wheel arches. Extra fresh-air ventilator and cabin-door ventilation (not with M60, M141, M505)	21–26		
191	With outer and centre underfloor plates	All		
193	With electrical installation for Japan: with side turn signals front, back-up lamps, with parking light front and rear, without licence-plate light and engine that complies to Japanese exhaust regulations (with M26 and M187 only)	21–23 (RHD)	1974–76	
194	Convex outer rear-view mirrors left and right instead of mirrors with flat glass	All	All	
195	Exlusive use of Blaupunkt car radios (with M95, 97 or 98 only)	21, 22, 23, 265, 27		
198	Rotating light red instead of blue (with M160 only)	All		
200	Various parts not mounted; these parts sent via the CKD department	221, 231, 261, 265		Yugoslavia
201	Pick-Up with enlarged wooden platform	261, 264	All	
203	Eberspächer BN4 petrol heater	265, 268	1968–73	
"	With second hot-air outlet in metal partition as in ambulance (with M500 only)	21, 23		
206	Inner rear-view mirror, anti-dazzle	All	1970–79	
207	Tilt and bows for Pick-Up	265, 268	All	
208	Trailer hitch and extra towing hook on front	All	1968–71	
"	Trailer hitch	All	1972–79	
209	Tilt made of PVC instead of sail-cloth (with M070 only)	261, 264		
"	Tilt made of PVC instead of sail-cloth (with M207 only)	265, 268		
211	With post horn sticker	21-26		German Mail – Berlin
212	With 'Fernmeldedienst' ('telecommunications department') and post horn stickers	21–26		German Mail – Berlin
213	Without rubber floor mat in passenger compartment	22, 24		United Kingdom
214	Detachable hinges and side-flap mountings	261, 265		For authorities only
215	Without air vents in cargo compartment (with M500 and M510 only)	211–216		
217	Flat bows with mountings for ladder and tilt made out of synthetic material	265		For authorities only

M-code	Description	Model type	Yrs/prd	Remarks
220	Limited slip differential	All	All	
221	One ventilation window in cabin door on driver's side	21, 23, 26, 27		
222	With fixed windows in passenger compartment instead of ventilation windows	231, 235	1968–71	
223	No window openings in passenger compartment	265, 268		
225	With upholstery on the boot floor, the sides of the boot and the rear hatch	231, 235		
226	Retaining cables for tailboard	26		
227	Detachable headrests for all seats in cabin (with M161 only)	All	1973–79	
229	Detachable headrests for all seats in passenger compartment (with M235 only)	22, 23, 24	1973–79	
235	Mountings for headrests for all seats in passenger compartment	22, 23, 24	1973–79	
240	Engine with recessed crown pistons for low-octane fuel	All	All	
243	Windscreen free from import duty for Canada (with M89 only)	21–26		Canada
246	Windscreen free from import duty for USA (with M89 only)	21–23 (LHD)		USA
248	Ignition lock without steering lock	All	1970–79	
249	Automatic transmission	21–24, 27	1973–79	
"	"	26	1976–79	
251	1700cc (66bhp) engine instead of 1600cc (50bhp)	21–24, 27	1972–73	
"	1800cc (68bhp) engine instead of 1600cc (50bhp)	21–23, 27	1974–75	
"	2000cc (70bhp) engine instead of 1600cc (50bhp)	All	1976–79	
252	1300cc (44bhp) engine instead of 1600cc (50bhp)	All	1971–75	Italy
253	Vehicle for North American market with tyres from specific companies	21, 22, 23 (LHD)		USA and Canada
257	Without spare tyre, tools, toolbag and jack (with M515/502 only)	211		Germany
258	Higher driver- and passenger-seat backrest (headrest)	All	1968–72	
259	Passenger seat instead of passenger bench seat; spare tyre in cabin (with M500 only)	211–216, 231–235, 265		
263	Payload of 1,200kg instead of 1,000kg	All	1974–79	
279	Maintenance vehicle for communication cables. With closets, C-shaped rails, swivel chair and curtains in cargo compartment (with M120, M503, M539 only; not with M251)	231		
288	With headlight washer installation	All	1974–79	
289	Sheer bolt for steering-column tube attachment			
300	Without bottom protection	All		
314	VW parts for type 214, 234 and 264 made by VW do Brasil (CKD only)	214, 234, 264		Only CKD vehicles
319	ECE regulations sticker 'R 10' (with M123 only) (suppression equipment for radio reception)	All		
320	ECE regulations sticker 'R 11' (door locks and hinges)	All		
322	ECE regulations sticker 'R 14' (seatbelt mountings)	22, 23, 27		
331	Without metal division between cabin and cargo compartment, passenger seat adjustable on rails	211, 231	1976–79	
332	Fitted with Semperit tyres	All		

M186, M525, M549.

M201.

M288.

53

Optional equipment (M-codes) (*continued*)

M-code	Description	Model type	Yrs/prd	Remarks
333	Fitted with Uniroyal tyres	21, 23, 26		
335	Special engine to comply with Austrian regulations (1600cc, 50bhp)	All	1976–79	Austria
338	With American parts and constructions for the Campmobile versions P21, P22 and P27; free of import duty (with M609 only)	231		
360–430	Model years 1968–69 – *see* table with group codes, page 61			
440	Prepared for the installation of a radio for LW, MW, SW, FM (not with M631)	21–27 (LHD)		
491	Neckarsulm CR car radio, with cassette player	All	1978	
"	Braunschweig CR car radio, with cassette player		1979	
500	Full-width metal partition between cabin and load compartment	21–23	All	
501	Two-person passenger seat instead of single passenger seat in cabin, spare tyre in left side of luggage compartment (not with M500)	21–24		
502	Hardboard interior side panels in cargo compartment	21–23	All	
503	Hardboard interior roof panels in cargo compartment	21–23	All	
504	Fresh-air duct to cargo compartment	21–23, 265, 268	All	
505	Hot-air outlet in front side of cargo compartment	21	All	
506	Brake servo and dual-circuit brake control lamp	All	1968–75	
"	Brake servo	All	1976–79	
507	Ventilation windows in cabin doors	21, 22, 23, 26, 27	All	
508	Ventilation window in sliding door and in all windows opposite sliding door in the passenger compartment (three windows in total)	22, 23, 24	1968–77	
"	Ventilation windows in sliding doors (two windows in total) (when ordered with M520)	22, 23, 24	1968–77	

M501.

M504.

M504.

M505.

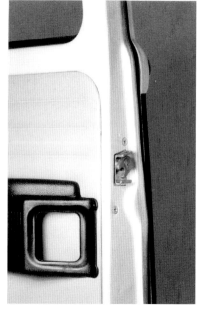

M504.

M506.

M-code	Description	Model type	Yrs/prd	Remarks
508	Ventilation window in rear passenger door and in the window opposite this door (two windows in total)	265, 268	All	
"	One sliding window in sliding door and one in the opposite side panel of the passenger compartment	22, 23	1978–79	
"	One sliding window in the side panel opposite the sliding door	23 (Westfalia Helsinki)	1978–79	
509	With dust-protected air intake, larger oil bath air cleaner and additional dust sealing	261–268	1968–74	
510	Upper division between cabin and cargo compartment	21	1968	
"	Upper division between cabin and cargo compartment. Fibreboard door panel in sliding door (Type 21: with air vents in rear side panels of cargo compartment)	21, 231	1969–79	
511	Padded dashboard and dashboard lid (not for RHD)	All (LHD)	All	
512	Without passenger seat in cabin			
513	Protection plate for gearbox	All		
514	Air circulation connection for gasoline heater (only with M119)	21–24, 27		
515	High roof Panelvan with high-roof sliding door	21		
516	High roof (plastic)	21	1968–71	

M506, 1968–72.

M507.

M508, 1968–77.

M508, 1978–79.

M515.

M510.

Optional equipment (M-codes) (*continued*)

M-code	Description	Model type	Yrs/prd	Remarks
516	High roof (plastic)	21, 23	1971–79	
517	Factory-prepared for Campmobile interior	231, 234		
518	Opening in roof with reinforcement for Westfalia pop-up roof	231, 234		
519	Air vents in cargo compartment (with M515 or 516 only)	211, 214		
520	With sliding door on left and right side	21–24	All	
521	With chrome trim and sun visor with mirror	22	1968–69	
"	With chrome trim and sun visor without mirror	22	1970–73	
522	Net division between cabin and cargo compartment	21–24		
524	USA and Canada specifications (*see also* page 64)	211–265	All	
525	Seatbelts for USA and Canada	211–265	1968–72	
526	Without inner rear-view mirror	All	1969	
527	Exhaust emission control system	All		Japan and Sweden
528	Convex rear-view mirror on right side (not for RHD)	All		
529	Upper partition between cabin and passenger compartment with sliding window (only with M500)	22, 23, 24		
530	Automatic step on passenger side (vehicles with two sliding doors only have the automatic step on the passenger side)	21–24		
531	Harder rear torsion bars (like on Transporter version) (on model 23 only with M013, 015, 146, 177 or 609)	22, 23, 24	1969–79	
533	Foot-operated alarm installation (for Taxis and rental vehicles)	22, 24	All	
534	Speaker and microphone for communication between driver and passengers	22, 24		
535	Tripwriter Diehl 'Co-Pilot' instead of standard speedometer (not in combination with M20)	All		
536	With rubber valve in rear bottom panel for draining fuel	21, 23, 27		Belgium
537	Transistor lamp instead of regular interior light	22, 24	1970–73	To chassis no. 2132 102 496
538	Interior with closets and wooden floor in the rear of the cabin, net partition between front and rear of cabin (with M117 only)	265		German Mail
539	Wooden floor in cargo compartment	211, 231		German Mail
540	Closets in cargo compartment and net partition between cabin and cargo compartment	211, 231		German Mail
541	Bench seat in upholstery cloth on metal partition behind cabin. Net division above closet but without net division between cabin and cargo compartment (with M503, M540 only)	231		German Mail
542	Various special constructions for German Army purposes (with M149 only. In case of model 265, with M101, M178, M207, M209 only)	231, 265, 271		German Army
543	Without seats in passenger compartment	22, 24		
544	High-roof Bus with shelves for piling packages in cargo compartment (with M502, M515 only)	211		
545	Headliner in load-/passenger compartment (as in model 22, Microbus)	23		
546	Turn signals at rear on roof	21–24, 27	1971–76	
"	Turn signals at rear on roof, lamp shines to both front and rear	21–23, 27	1977–79	
547	Extra rust-prevention treatment	All		
549	Three-point safety belts for driver and outer passenger seat, two-point safety belt for middle seat (only in case of two-person passenger seat in cabin)	All	1974–79	
551	Halogen headlamps	All		
557	Clock with heating time preselector, with trip counter (with M060 only)	All (LHD)	1974–79	
560	Steel sliding roof	22, 23	All	
568	Tinted windows (except windscreen)(with M671 only)	22, 23	1974–75	
"	Tinted windows and windscreen, with laminated windscreen	22, 23	1976–77	
569	Air filter for dusty countries (2000cc with 70bhp only)	All		South Africa and Australia
571	Rear foglamp	All	1973–79	
573	Airconditioning (on model 23 only for Campers)(with M251 only)	22, 23 (LHD)	1974–75	

M557.

TOP: *M517 and M518.*　　　　ABOVE: *M530.*

M546, 1968–76.　　　　*M546, 1977–79.*　　　　*M571.*

Optional equipment (M-codes) (*continued*)

M-code	Description	Model type	Yrs/prd	Remarks
575	Preparation for construction of Campmobile by Jurgens-Caravan in South Africa or Karmann Mobil in Germany	211, 214		
583	Without compressor for folding spare tyre (with M586 only)	231		
585	Interior panel over entire width of vehicle for lower partition between cabin and cargo compartment	211, 214		
586	With folding spare tyre instead of regular spare tyre, plus 12V air compressor and 12V connection on dashboard	231, 234		Westfalia Campmobile
587	Hannover radio (LW, MW, FM) with automatic search, remote control, tape deck and automatic antenna connection	All	1972–74	
"	Salzgitter radio (FM) with tape player connection and traffic broadcast decoder connection	All	1976–79	
597	Stronger battery: 12V 63A instead of 12V 45A	All		
600	Comfort package			
601	Special options package comprising: back-up lamps (M047); rear-window defroster (M102); emergency warning lights; dual-circuit brake warning light; padded dashboard (for LHD)	211–268, 271	1968	
602	Special options package comprising: hazard lights; dual-circuit brake warning light; padded dashboard (for LHD)	211–268	1968	
603	Deluxe version (with M025, M162, M507, M616 only. In case of 1600cc engine, M171)	221, 224		
606	2000cc dual carburettor engine with secondary air injection	21, 22, 23, 26 (RHD)		
608	Compliance with Australian exhaust and safety standards	All (RHD)	1976–79	
609	Westfalia Campmobile	231, 234	1972–79	
612	Without diagnosis plug connection and wiring	All		
614	Adjustment mechanism for later gauging of speedometer (for rental vehicles and self-drive rentals only)	All (LHD)		
616	Reversing lights (built-in with rearlight units)	21–26	1972–79	
618	Generator 70A instead of 55A (with M157 or M251 only)	All	1975–79	
623	Special suppression equipment, prepared for radio-traffic	All	All	
628	'Commando vehicle equipment' also useable as conversation vehicle, bureau vehicle and for similar purposes. Consisting of three-seater middle bench seat (built-in facing backwards); folding down backrest on sliding door side; one folding table; one transistorized light above table; one rubber floor cover in passenger compartment	231, 235	1973–79	
629	Mounting for radio-communication apparatus in glovebox, model Telefunken 7b or SEL	21–27 (LHD)	1973–79	
631	Suppressed windscreen-wiper motor	All		
632	Further suppressed equipment	All		German Army
634	Windscreen-wiper blades and arms under customs seal	211, 221, 231		
640	'Air-drying' bottom protection instead of 'wax paraffin'	All		
647	With USA-specific parts for the airconditioning (free from import duty)	221, 231		USA
652	Interval switch on windscreen wipers and wash-wipe installation. Interval *ca.* 6 seconds	All	1973–79	
659	Two halogen foglamps on front	All	1973–79	
663	Stick-in head-/neck-rests. Not for driver's seat	214, 224, 234, 264, 274		Japan
664	Sticker ECE regulations no. 14	All		Belgium
671	Tinted windscreen (laminated) (with M568 only)	22, 23	1974–75	
673	Sealed speedometer (for leasing vehicles)	All		
677	Workshop vehicle for Deutsche Bundespost (German Mail) with C-shaped rails and net partition between cargo compartment and cabin (with M500, M502, M539 only)	211		German Mail
679	Interior as M677 with extra built-in closets and extractable vice (only with M677)	211		
688	Motorola/USA car radio instead of Emden (with M097 only)	211, 221, 231		

M659.

M690.

M-code	Description	Model type	Yrs/prd	Remarks
689	Workshop vehicle for Deutsche Bundespost (German Mail) with C-shaped rails and net partition between cargo compartment and cabin, with extra built-in closets and vice (with M500, M502, M539 only)	231		German Mail
690	Passenger seat in cabin as swivelling seat, without metal partition behind this seat	211, 221, 231, 234	1976–79	Chassis no. 2162 078 000 and up
697	Fitted with Continental-manufactured tyres	21–26		
700–799	*See* table of 'S-codes', below			
912	Without chassis identification plate			
920	With protection wall in cargo compartment	21		
935	Transistorized ignition system	211, 221, 231	1979	USA-California
966	Polyester high roof painted in body colour instead of white (with M515 or M516 only)	21, 23	1979	

S-CODES

The M-code range 700–799 was reserved for the so-called 'S-codes' ('s' as in *Sonderausführung*, or 'special body'). S-codes (*see* pages 60–1) were applied for special built-ins or for special labour that had to be done on the Buses during production. In Volkswagen literature the numbers in the 700–799 range are written with an 'S' in front of them, instead of the 'M' for M-code.

GROUP CODES

Codes that start with a letter usually stand for a group of M-codes, in some cases for a specific SO interior. Volkswagen had two reasons to start clustering M-codes together in one other code. First, certain export markets required special extras as standard equipment, and it was more sensible to print one code on the plate rather than to fill up the space with the same codes for every Bus going in the direction of that market.

The second reason was the increasing amount of optional equipment that was becoming available. On a highly equipped Bus, the M-codes simply would not fit on the plate any more; this is clear on many plates of the late 1970s.

In the first two model years (1968 and 1969) the group codes are mentioned as M-codes in the range M360–M430. By the end of the 1960s it had become clear that these seventy possibilities could not cover the increasing number of package variations. With the introduction of model year 1970, Volkswagen decided to switch to letters to identify the different groups of codes. First, it was only one letter and two digits ('L15', for example), but by the end of the 1970s the range of variations had become so wide that virtually every combination had to be used. In

addition, in each model year these group codes were 're-issued', resulting in a completely different list – the references began to seem never-ending. For this reason only the most commonly used group codes are given here.

In 1973 four standard packages were introduced, which lasted for the remaining production years. These codes all start with a 'Z'. They represent Bad Weather Packages, for weather-related equipment such as a rear-window defroster and foglamps, and the M-Package, for a set of luxury extras. These group codes are listed separately here, since they are the same for each model year from 1973 until 1979.

SO CONVERSIONS

If an SO conversion was applied to a vehicle, Volkswagen sometimes made use (*continued on page 64*)

S-codes

S-code	Description	Model type	Yrs/prd	Remarks
703	Without side and rear windows in passenger compartment (preparation for Westfalia isolation windows)	231	1979	
705	Zeiss-Ikon safety lock for rear panel lid (available with M145, one key combination)	21	1970	
"	Airconditioning	22–24	1973	
710	Tail-light lenses yellow-red instead of yellow-red-white	21–23, 26	1972–79	German Mail
711	Without air vents in cargo compartment			
712	Factory-prepared for conversion to armoured money transporter (conversion by Thiele in Bremen)	21		
718	Illuminated roof sign with Maltese or Red Cross logo	21–23	All	
719	Production number for special, documented build-ins	26	1978	
723	Special sales campaign for 'Champagne Edition', paint colour Agata Brown with Atlas White roof; interior cloth in Parchment (beige grey)	221	1977	USA
728	Chrome trim around Bus *ca.* 5cm below windows	231	1974	Westfalia Campmobiles
729	Textile radial tyres with tube		1969–70	
734	2000cc fuel-injected engine with exhaust emission control concept of the 1800cc engine (with M157 only)	211, 221, 231		
736	Alternative loading arrangement (not with S751)	27		
737	Without portable chair but with guiding rails on floor	27		
741	Window in sliding door (in case of double sliding door, there is a window in both sliding doors)	211, 215		
743	Without right stretcher and without right loading platform	27		
"	Factory-prepared for fitting a PVC tilt	26		
744	Wooden floor panels with built-in guide rails for mounting tools and instruments (only with M502 or bench seats)		1970–71	
745	Control number for conversions or other changes from the serial production			
751	Two head cushions, one back support, one belly support, guiding rail lock for stretcher; without infusion hooks	27		
753	Sliding door right instead of left (RHD vehicles)	RHD		
756	Window in sliding door and one at opposite side panel	211, 215		
758	Production number to indicate small special build-ins or deflections from the serial production	26		
759	With upholstery on floor above engine, the rear corners and the rear hatch (with M013, 015, 146 or 177 only)	23	1970	

S728.

S777.

S756.

S-code	Description	Model type	Yrs/prd	Remarks
759	70bhp engine	21–26 (RHD)	1976	Australia, chassis nos. 2162 119 000 to 2162 164 000
761	Upper fibreboard partition (with M013, 015, 146 or 177 only)	231, 235		
762	Seats and interior panels in black			
765	Special sales campaign for 'Champagne Edition II'	221, 231	1978	USA
766	Special sales campaign for 'Silberfisch' (Germany)	221	1978–79	Germany
768	Illuminated roof sign with Maltese Cross logo	271	1979	
769	Without sliding door; in case of double sliding door version (M520), both sliding doors left out			
777	Preparation for later installation of UTILA stretcher	22, 23		
779	Ventilation window in cabin door on driver's side			
786	Sliding roof for RHD	234		
791	Preparation for later installation of UTILA stretcher	231	1973–79	
793	Production number indicating a special note in the German licence papers, saying that a Trumatic SB 2000 gas heater has been fitted	231	1977–79	Westfalia Campmobiles
795	Sliding door left instead of right	LHD		

Group codes

1968–69

Code	M-codes represented	Code	M-codes represented
360	090 106 156 220 240 507	396	008 020 061 196
361	010 056 075 240	397	123 124
362	020 024 090	398	008 075
363	106 156 240	399	008 075 120
364	056 094 121 240 507 508	400	056 121 507 623
365	056 092 109 121 208 219 220	401	056 090 101 507 623
366	056 090 101 194	402	013 056 111
367	013 056 066 090 106 121 623	403	036 090
368	020 196	404	056 121 507
369	106 124 156	405	013 056 181
370	020 024	406	013 056 092 109 121 219 623
371	056 092 109 121 208 219 220 623	407	020 094 106 196 240 156
372	013 056 066 090 121 149 623	408	010 075 090 106 240 156
373	013 056 066 090 149	409	056 065 145 507 602 729
374	056 090 101 121 507 508	410	056 089 121 181
375	010 056 075 094 106 121	411	008 020 089 196
376	056 101 121 156 194 220 240 (until 12.1967)	412	056 601
379	010 029 056 156 194 240 623	415	050 089 511 528
380	075 092 094 121 240 508	418	056 092 220
381	056 090 601	419	065 109 207 208 214 217
382	094 106 156 196	420	018 029 056 (1968)
384	056 065 507 510	420	055 119 520 530 (1969)
385	109 159 502	421	018 029 047 056 121 194
386	029 056 101 121 181 601 623 718	422	010 056 106 121 196 623
387	056 109 121	423	056 106 181 220 507
388	020 090 511 524	425	020 089 507 511 524
389	056 121 208 507 508	426	020 089 511 524
390	020 101 106 181 196 507	427	056 065 111 207
391	056 109 121 502 503	428	106 156 507
393	056 090 106 181 507	429	056 092 094 101 240 507
394	047 056 065 127 181 507 602 729	430	013 090 106 156 220 240 503 507 508
395	056 623		

(continued overleaf)

Group codes (*continued*)

1970

Code	M-codes represented
C01	020 089 102 181 206 507 511 517 524 525
C65	094 156 507
C75	047 507
C77	500 510
C88	020 089 206 507 511 524 525
C89	020 089 102 206 507 511 521 524 525
C96	020 061 187
C97	037 123 124
D25	020 089 102 206 507 511 521 524 525
D26	020 089 102 206 511 524 525
D46	032 047 050 094 208 511
D65	032 047 050 094 208 248 511
E82	029 092 220
F93	121 206 511
G22	020 032 089 094 103 206 507 511 513
L15	032 094 120 248

1971

Code	M-codes represented
A01	020 026 089 102 206 506 507 511 521 524 525
A02	020 026 089 102 206 506 511 524 525
A05	047 507
A06	500 510
A07	150 151 514 623
A18	032 047 094 102 507
A19	020 026 089 102 181 206 506 507 511 517 524 525
A41	020 061 187
A42	037 123 124
A44	062 089 094 506 511
B24	103 121 506 507
E48	032 047 094 181 206 507
N67	020 026 089 102 113 181 206 506 507 511 524 525
N93	020 094 102 187 206 506 507 793

1972

Code	M-codes represented
A01	020 026 089 102 206 506 507 511 521 524 525
A02	020 026 089 102 206 506 511 524 525
A03	020 026 089 506 507 511 524 525
A05	507 616
A07	150 151 623
A41	020 061 187
A44	062 089 094 506 511
B18	074 094 206 616
B55	074 506 507 616
D01	094 172 506 507 623
H38	020 026 089 206 506 511 524 525
K09	094 102 507 616 623
K10	032 054 089 094 102 121 172 506 507 511
K13	089 172 181 206 506 507 511 616
K42	020 026 089 102 181 185 206 506 507 511 521 524
K43	020 026 089 102 185 206 506 511 524
K44	020 026 089 185 206 506 511 524
K45	020 026 089 185 506 507 511 524
K46	020 026 089 102 181 185 206 506 507 511 524
K47	020 026 089 181 185 206 506 507 511 524

(continued)

Code	M-codes represented
K48	020 026 089 102 113 181 185 206 506 507 511 524
L08	008 094 248 507

1973

Code	M-codes represented
A05	507 616
A06	500 510
A13	065 507 616
A29	065 500 510 616
A41	020 061 085 187
A44	062 085 089 094 506 511
A97	074 616
C25	020 089 102 161 185 206 506 507 511 524
C48	082 083 085 106 121 171 502 503 508 615
D03	020 068 089 102 113 141 161 172 185 206 235 506 507 511 524
D04	020 068 085 089 102 172 185 206 506 511 524
D06	020 068 085 089 102 161 172 185 206 506 511 524
D07	020 068 085 089 113 161 172 181 185 206 506 507 511 524
D09	020 068 089 102 141 161 185 206 235 506 507 511 524
D10	020 068 089 102 161 172 185 206 506 511 524
D12	020 068 089 102 161 185 206 235 506 511 524
D13	020 068 089 102 161 185 206 506 511 524
D14	020 068 089 102 161 185 206 235 506 511 524
D15	020 068 089 102 161 185 206 506 511 524
D30	020 085 089 102 113 161 172 181 185 206 253 506 507 511 524
D31	020 085 089 102 161 172 185 206 253 506 511 524
D32	020 085 089 102 141 161 185 206 235 253 506 511 524
D33	020 085 089 102 161 185 206 235 253 506 511 524
D34	020 085 089 161 172 185 206 253 506 511 524
D35	020 085 089 113 161 172 185 253 506 507 511 524
D36	020 089 102 113 141 161 172 185 206 235 253 506 507 511 524
D37	020 085 089 113 161 172 181 185 206 253 506 507 511 524
D38	020 085 089 102 161 185 206 253 506 511 524
D39	020 085 089 102 161 172 185 206 253 506 511 524

1974

Code	M-codes represented
A06	500 510
A28	124 506
A41	020 061 085 187
AH2	161 181 227 506 511
BV9	032 089 094 102 161 181 206 227 506 511
D52	020 068 085 089 102 161 185 206 235 253 506 507 511 524
D55	020 068 085 089 102 161 172 181 185 206 253 506 511 524 586
D58	020 068 085 089 102 113 161 172 181 185 206 506 507 511 524
EK2	082 094 100 102 121 161 181 184 194 206 506 511 551 568 671
GY3	102 161 181 506 511 568 652 671

1975

Code	M-codes represented
A41	020 061 085 187
A52	094 103 124 153 240
A90	102 506 507
D02	067 068 085 089 102 161 185 206 235 253 506 507 511 524
D05	005 012 067 085 089 102 161 172 181 185 206 253 506 511 524
D08	020 085 089 102 113 161 172 181 185 206 253 506 507 511 524
FH7	008 094 120 123
NF9	032 089 172

1976

Code	M-codes represented
A20	032 094
A34	123 506 507 528
A35	120 123 500 506 507 528
A36	120 123 506 507 528
A37	123 500 506 507 528
A38	123 226 506 507 528
A41	020 061 085 187
B30	050 123 506 507 528
B50	065 085 089 100 101 103 121 149 191 549
C02	094 172 184 206 506 511
C12	032 094 102
CFX	074 172
D50	012 067 102 508
D51	012 067 102 148 508
D52	012 067 102 206 235
D53	005 012 067 102
D54	020 060 102 113 597 618
FS9	032 094 102
H86	050 507
L10	032 050 102 203

1977

Code	M-codes represented
A25	050 085 123 506 507 528 697 912
A40	161 181 511
A75	184 335 506 912
A76	184 506 912
A93	184 506 912
B30	050 123 506 507 528
B33	050 062 085 086 089 094 102 123 161 288 319 506 511 616 618
CK6	161 206 227
CSH	032 089 506 511 597 618
CUN	032 054 073 094 103 181
D01	012 067 102 508
D03	005 012 067 102 206 235
D04	002 012 067 102 206
D09	012 067 102 162 227 508 723
E19	089 161 184 227
G23	050 172 184 506 511
GR0	089 100 121 161 172 623
GU9	161 171 181 184 227
H64	161 172 181 184 227
L84	054 103 106 184
NU9	065 085 127 184 191
S98	032 082 094 103 503 551
SF9	074 551
SR3	082 100 102 103 106 161 172

1978

Code	M-codes represented
A23	050 085 123 506 507 528 697 912
A51	020 061 085 187 194
A83	123 124 172 506
B32	123 571 912

CN9	066 082 089 102 186
D50	012 067 102 508
D51	012 067 102 206
D52	012 067 102
D59	060 073 102 113 121 123 597 618
D60	060 102 113 121 123 597 618
D61	012 067 102 162 508 568 652 765
D63	012 067 102 162 568 652 765
E81	184 227 506 511
FB0	032 089 094 161
FRB	032 094 172
GU2	121 161 172 184 227 623
H40	161 181 506 511
KS2	065 089 103 127 191
N06	085 120 123
N39	184 186 207 209 227
R32	032 060 082 085 094 100
RS6	032 065 082 085 089
RS7	100 101 103 121 149 161
S32	032 060 094 102
V19	161 184 227 511
W50	032 054 082 096 102 161 172 184 206 227 235 511 551 560
W51	508 733 766

1979

Code	M-codes represented
A51	020 061 085 187 194
A67	061 085 123 172 194 506
A81	050 085 123 506 507 528 697 912
A82	050 085 123 506 528 697 912
A83	025 032 054 073 089 094 120 161 172 181 511
A84	050 085 123 506 697 912
A85	050 085 123 194 697 912
A86	050 085 194 697 912
A87	123 571 912
CT8	032 065 089 100 103 161
D01	012 067 102 508
D02	012 067 102 206 235
D03	012 067 073 102
D27	027 935
EUR	032 089 094 551
FCY	032 089 094 161 172
FVN	161 172 181 184 227 506 511
G17	161 172 184 227
HAT	186 690
L28	089 161 184 506
L68	032 094 100 102
NE5	181 511
R45	032 094 102 161 206
R65	032 094 102 506
RY6	032 085 149 178 186
S52	032 089 094 161
TL3	082 085 101 121 149
TL4	178 184 186 191 207
W50	032 054 082 096 102 161 172 184 206 227 235 511 551 560
W51	508 733 766

(continued overleaf)

Group codes (*continued*)

Group codes starting with 'Z' (1973–1979)

Code	M-codes represented
Z01	Bad-weather package 1: rear foglamp (M571); wiper switch with interval option (M652); two halogen foglamps on front (M659)
Z02	Bad-weather package 2: rear-window defroster (M102); wiper switch with interval option (M652); two halogen foglamps on front (M659)

Code	M-codes represented
Z05	M-package: trip km counter and clock (M025); rubber mouldings on bumpers front and back (M162); ventilation windows in cabin doors (M507); back-up lamps (M616)
Z21	Z01 and Z05 together (M025 162 507 571 616 652 659)

SO conversions

1968–70

Code	Conversion	Models
A03	SO3, VW Kombi as traffic accident observation vehicle	23
A67	SO67, Westfalia Campmobile 67A	23
B67	SO67, Westfalia Campmobile 67B	23
	As interior 67A but with additional pop-up roof, bed and built-in roof luggage rack	
D67	SO67, Westfalia Campmobile 67D	23
	As interior 67B but with additional tent	
E67	SO67, Westfalia Campmobile 67E	23
F67	SO67, Westfalia Campmobile 67F	23
G67	SO67, Westfalia Campmobile 67G	23
H67	SO67, Westfalia Campmobile 67H	23

1971–79

Code	Conversion	Models
P10	VW Kombi as traffic accident vehicle	23
P11	VW Kombi as traffic accident vehicle with additional roof platform and ladder	23
P20	Double-seater middle bench and special rear bench	22, 23
P21	Campmobile without pop-up roof, with folding spare tyre	231
P22	Campmobile with pop-up roof, with folding spare tyre	231
P23	Campmobile with pop-up roof	231
P24	Campmobile with pop-up roof and combined gas/electric refrigerator	231
P25	Campmobile with pop-up roof	234
P26	Campmobile with pop-up roof and combined gas/electric refrigerator	234
P27	Campmobile Deluxe with pop-up roof, folding spare tyre, combined gas/electric refrigerator (1976–79)	231
P28	With additional tent for P21 to P27	231, 234
P29	With additional electricity inlet for 220V. For P25 and P26	234
P30	1971–73: Westfalia interior (without pop-up roof)	23
"	1976–79: Combined gas/electric refrigerator, with gas cooking unit, side bench in driving direction for storing gas bottles. For P21 and P22.	231
P31	Westfalia with pop-up roof	23
P32	Additional tent for interior P31	23

of a specific code that – like the group codes – also started with a letter. In the early years (1968–70), the number indicated the SO version and the letter the variation to this conversion. A clear example are the codes for the Westfalia Campmobile SO67. A67 is the code for the standard version while B67 indicates some additional camping equipment. In model year 1970 it became slightly more confusing, as Volkswagen had also started to use letters in the group codes. From 1971 onwards the letter 'P' was reserved for SO conversions.

ADDITIONAL INFORMATION ON M-CODES

M65 (Text for Maximum Axle Loads and Maximum Weight)

According to German law, all commercial vehicles must have the maximum axle loads marked above the wheels and the maximum total mass on the front of the car. The maximum total weight is printed on the left lower part of the front of the car. The maximum front-axle load is printed to the top left of the right wheel arch. The maximum rear-axle load is printed above the wheel arch of the right rear wheel.

These maximum loads vary from model year to model year. M263 'Payload of 1,200kg instead of 1,000kg' also plays a role in the amounts. If the printing has gone missing over the years, they may be found on the ID plate behind the passenger seat.

M511 – Padded Dashboard

In January 1967 the padded dashboard became compulsory on US vehicles. The Split Window Bus was not yet available with this option, but, when the T2 was introduced in August 1967, so was the padded dashboard. Each Bus for the USA and Canada had M511. In the rest of the world the T2 dashboard still had a steel surface; the padded version could be ordered at extra cost and was only available for LHD vehicles. Particularly in the early years, few customers bought this optional extra with their Bus.

M524 (Canada and USA Specifications)

In the 1960s, US traffic-safety regulations for new vehicles were much more stringent than in the rest of the world. North America was a very important market for Volkswagen, so the German

M65, front panel.

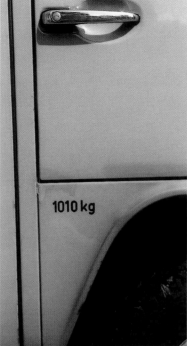

M65, front wheel.

M65, rear wheel.

M511.

Above the tail-lights are the back-up lamps. In most countries an optional extra (M47), this was standard as part of M524 for the USA and Canada.

Further electrical modifications include a buzzer that reminds the driver to take the keys out of the ignition on opening the driver's door. A red warning lamp installed near the speedo warns the driver in case the pressure in the dual-circuit brake system drops. With model year 1973, illuminated symbols appeared at the hot-/fresh-air levers on the dashboard panel. This was done because of new legal requirements. This type of dashboard illumination can be found only on Buses that were meant to be sold in the USA or Canada.

The US authorities required the chassis number to be visible through the windscreen, so all US Buses have a plate with the chassis number on top of the dashboard. A vehicle safety certificate sticker is fixed in the door jamb on the driver's side. It shows the month and year of manufacture, the chassis number and asserts that the vehicle conforms to regulations. In later years this sticker took over the function of the chassis plate, and therefore the plate disappeared from these vehicles.

Microbuses (Type 22) were additionally equipped with a chrome VW logo on the front and chrome trim around the windows.

The Pick-Up versions (Type 26) got two round openings in the tailboard. This way the tail-lights are visible when the tailgate is opened. In 1971, however, VW stopped delivering Pick-Ups to the USA because of tax regulations on commercial vehicles.

M524 evolved continuously over the years and the table (*see* page 66) shows an overview of the changes.

manufacturer did everything to comply with these rules, and developed a range of equipment especially designed for the North American market. M524 comprises most of the optional extras that were standard on North American Buses and a few items that are unique to this export market. During the years the meaning of the code also changed.

In August 1969, the side marker reflectors changed from circle-shaped to square, and at the same time the red side reflectors on the rear were equipped with a lamp. M524 also involves modifications to the electrical system. In the USA and Canada, sealed-beam headlamps are used, giving a different beam of light from the standard (European) headlamp units. The front turn signal indicators are equipped with a duplo bulb, the faint light in which replaces the parking lights found on European Buses. The stronger light in the turn signal units burns when the turn signal lever is operated or when the hazard light switch is pulled. Until August 1971 the oval rear lamps had one duplo bulb, with the regular tail-light and a stronger light that burns either when the brakes are applied or when the turn signals are on. The lens is completely red and is held in position by a chrome rim.

M524. Side marker reflector front 1968–69.

M524. Side marker reflector rear 1970–79.

M524. Reversing light and all-red tail-light lens with chrome rim 1968–71.

M524. Side marker reflector rear 1968–69.

M524. Side marker reflector front 1970–79.

Overview of the M524 specifications

Description		Period
Electrical		
Side marker reflectors	round	1968–1969
	square with lamp in rear reflector	1970–1979
Sealed-beam headlamps		All model years
All red tail-light lenses with chrome rim		1968–1971
Front turn signal lenses with duplo bulb		All model years
Dual-circuit brake warning lamp		All model years
Ignition key warning buzzer		1970–1979
Illuminated fresh-/hot-air symbols		1973–1979
Other		
Chassis number behind windscreen		All model years
Vehicle safety certificate sticker		All model years
No chassis plate behind passenger seat		1976–79
Type 22 (Microbus)		
Chrome trim around windows		All model years
Chrome VW logo on front		All model years
Type 26 (Pick-Up single-cab and crew-cab)		
Circular opening in tailboard		1968–71

paint and interior colours

Very few vehicles have been produced in as many different colours as the T2. Although regular customers had a limited choice in terms of the colour in which their Bus could be delivered, companies or local authorities could order special coloured Buses to suit their own style. The alternative to this procedure was to order a primered vehicle and then have it painted by a local paint shop.

BODY AND ROOF COLOURS

The standard colours were listed in the back of every Transporter brochure and a regular vehicle was painted in one colour all over. When ordering a Microbus, a coloured roof was available at extra cost. With a Microbus Deluxe, a two-coloured body was standard. During the production years of the T2, the most common roof colour available was white. The Microbus body would be painted all over in the main colour, then its roof would be painted afterwards in Cloud White L581. Until model year 1970, the border between the two colours was the rain gutter.

The process changed with the start of model year 1971. First of all the body of a two-tone Bus would be painted entirely in Pastel White L90D, then a second colour would be applied on the lower half of the outside of the Bus. The border between the two colours was lowered to the body profile, which lies approximately 10cm below the windows.

In model year 1971 Black L41 also became available as roof colour. This colour combination was not very popular and the option was removed from the regular sales programme the following year.

In the late 1970s the Microbus series was enriched with a few more colour combinations. Model year 1978 brought Dakota Beige L13A as a roof colour, available only in combination with Agate

Two-tone paint job 1968–70. Border in rain gutter.

Two-tone paint job 1971–79. Border under belt line.

Brown L86Z. One year later, in the last model year of the T2, Dakota Beige was replaced by Mexico Beige LE1M. The new beige tone was available with Sage Green L63H or Agate Brown L86Z.

WHEELS, FITMENTS AND CARGO COMPARTMENT

Wheels were painted Cloud White L581. Deluxe models had Black L41 wheels. In 1971 the design of the wheel changed, due to the introduction of disc brakes. From this year on, the wheels on all models were chrome-coloured (L91).

Bumpers for 1968–70 vehicles were Cloud White L581. Ambulances had Ivory L567 coloured bumpers. From 1971 onwards, all bumpers, including those of the Ambulance, were Pastel White L90D. In 1973 new, square-shaped bumpers were introduced. These late-model bumpers were chromed on Deluxe Microbuses.

Hubcaps were painted Grey Silver L70X as standard, but from 1971 onwards they were finished in chrome colour L91, the same as the wheel. Chrome hubcaps were fitted on the standard Microbus, on the Microbus Deluxe and on the Ambulance. A regular Transporter could also be fitted with chrome hubcaps as an optional extra (M181).

The front badge was Cloud White L581 until 1970. From 1971 onwards it was Pastel White L90D. Chrome logos were fitted on Deluxe models or as an optional extra (M181 or M521).

The load compartment of the Panelvans and Kombis was Dark Grey L74X until November 1967. From chassis number 218 059 935 onwards, the cargo area was painted Light Beige L275.

The steering-column tube, gearshift and handbrake lever were Black L41 for all model years.

Seat frames came in Grey Black L43 in all years and models.

SPECIAL PAINT JOBS (*SONDERLACKIERUNGEN*)

Customers who ordered a number of Bay Window Buses with the same specifications could have them delivered with special paint options – perhaps company colours. It was also possible to fulfil more specific requirements, such as having the roof or other body

Pattern of regular seat, vertical lines 1968–72.   *Pattern of regular seat, no lines 1973–79.*

sections done in a different colour. Other parts, such as wheels, hubcaps and bumpers, could also be ordered in a different colour. In some cases, a special paint job was applied when a customer wanted an old VW colour that was no longer available via the regular paint programme. It is not always possible to find any great detail on this subject, however, as Volkswagen did not always record it in the archives.

Factory-delivered Westfalia Campmobiles also have a *Sonderlackierung*, but often the body is a plain VW colour used in the model year the Bus was produced. The reason for this lies in the inside of the Bus. A Westfalia Camper is based on a VW Transporter – a delivery van with windows, painted grey or beige in the cargo compartment – and Westfalia wanted the interior of the Bus painted in the body colour. A special painting instruction was therefore required for these vehicles and that is why a *Sonderlackierung* was applied.

INTERIOR

Seats and Door Panels

The material of the seat covers in most Buses is leatherette, a long-lasting material that is easily cleaned. VW documentation does not distinguish between the seat covers of the luxury Microbus and those of the standard Microbus and company vehicles, but there is a very clear difference in the materials. With the regular leatherette, the seat and backrest are covered in a plastic-like material while the material used in the Deluxe Buses is more

like real leather. The sides and the back of the seats in all cases are covered in vinyl.

A more comfortable cloth interior was also available. This applied only to the seat and backrest area, while the rest of the seat cover and the interior panels remained the same as with leatherette.

Regular leatherette seats have a plait pattern on the seat and backrest. In the early years of the Bay Window, vertical lines were added. With the beginning of model year 1973 these lines were removed. The seats of the standard Microbus and the Deluxe have a ladder pattern in them.

Dual-Coloured Interiors

Dual-coloured interiors were available for Microbuses in the years 1968–70. The door and side panels were dual-coloured and so were the seats. The border between the two colours on the seats depends on the type of Microbus. The standard Microbus (Type 22) had

Dual-coloured interior on standard Microbus 1968–70.

Dual-coloured interior on deluxe Microbus 1968–70.

the whole seating area plus the backrest area in the lighter colour, with the sides in a darker colour. On the Deluxe Microbus (Type 24) the light area is much smaller and in the passenger compartment each seating place is marked by the light colour.

The dual-coloured interior was available in Light Grey/Medium Grey and Light Sand/Khaki Brown. The latter came with floor mats, kick panels, luggage-compartment carpeting and a spare-tyre cover in Khaki Brown instead of the standard black.

Ambulance

The factory-built Ambulances (Type 27) were equipped with a Medium Grey interior, to comply with German DIN specifications for Ambulances. These also required the seat covers to have a smooth surface instead of the plait pattern used on the regular leatherette covers.

Westfalia Campmobile

The cabin of the Westfalia Campmobile was fitted with standard seats and door panels until 1973. This means a Beige interior for 1968 models and Dark Beige interior from 1969 to 1973. From 1974 onwards Westfalias were equipped with cabin seats that matched the plaid upholstery used in the Camper interior. The side parts of the seats, the door-panels and the optional headrests were delivered in a single colour and had a smooth surface with no cloth involved.

Commercial Vehicles

The regular company vehicles (Panelvans, Pick-Ups and Kombis) were usually available in one interior colour only. Depending on the model year, this was

Beige (1968), Dark Beige (1969–76) or Canyon Brown (1977–79).

Alternatives to the standard Dark Beige were available for Panelvans produced in the period February 1975 until January 1976. The alternative colours were Slate, Juniper (green) and Lapis Blue. Slate lasted a full year in the production programme but Juniper and Lapis Blue were both cancelled after a few months, and are very rare nowadays.

COLOUR IDENTIFICATION

Details of the original paint colour can be found on the sticker fixed on the metal partition behind the driver's seat (passenger seat on RHD vehicles). Initially, the paint sticker was applied only when the vehicle was painted in a colour from the regular VW programme. From model year 1978 onwards cars with a special colour also got a paint sticker.

The sticker has a grey surface with black letters, and was made of paper, which is the reason why, in many cases, it has gone missing during the years. If the sticker is no longer legible, the original colour can still be identified from the M-plate. The M-plate also gives information on the upholstery that was used. The codes that represent the body colour are the first and second numbers on the third line. The roof colour is shown in the third and fourth numbers and the colour of the interior can be ascertained from the fifth and sixth numbers.

The exceptions to this rule are the cases of special paint jobs, or *Sonderlackierungen* in German. Until model year 1971, these codes were six digits long, making it impossible to fit the interior code there as well. Therefore, a Bus with a *Sonderlackierung* had a standard interior. In 1968 models this was Beige; during 1969, 1970 and 1971, the standard interior was Dark

Beige. A black interior was available by ordering option S762 (*see* Chapter 7). Microbuses would be finished with an interior matching the body colour.

Reading the codes can be a bit complicated, so a few examples are given below for clarification:

- standard paint code: most Buses would carry a standard sort of code, for example, P4P477. The first 'P4' indicates body colour Sage Green L63H; the second 'P4', roof colour Sage Green L63H; '77' means interior material leatherette, colour Canyon Brown;
- two-tone paint code: a two-tone Microbus could have a code like P4R177, which should be read as body colour Sage Green L63H ('P4'); roof colour Pastel White L90D ('R1'); interior material leatherette, colour Canyon Brown ('77');
- special paint job 1968–71: Buses with a *Sonderlackierung* of model years 1968–71 have a code that looks like this: 521614. This should be read as follows: '5' indicates that the Bus had a *Sonderlackierung* or special paint job; '21' means that the paint colour was used on a VW Type 21 (in other words, a VW Panelvan); '614' indicates that the *Sonderlackierung* was no. 614, in other words, Police Green L217 (RAL 6009);
- special paint job 1972–79: from model year 1972 on, a four-digit *Sonderlackierung* code was used, so that there was also room for the interior code. So, for example, 961477 means the following: '9' shows that the Bus had a special paint job; '614' indicates that the *Sonderlackierung* was no. 614, in other words, Police Green L217 (RAL 6009); '77' shows that the

Typical paint sticker, located behind driver's seat, RHD: passenger seat.

interior material was leatherette, colour Canyon Brown.

REGULAR PAINT CODES

The table below shows the codes of the colours that were available to regular customers. Of course, not all colours were available at the same time, as the colour programme changed through the years to match the current fashions. In addition, not all colours were available on every model. Some colour combinations were specific to the Microbus, while others were delivered on Transporters only. A few colours related to a special sales campaign and were applied only to the Buses that were part of those campaigns.

The colour code printed on the M-plate is a number that was used only on the form that was sent to the factory when a vehicle was ordered, and then on the M-plate. For this reason, these codes can also be found in most brochures. For repainting purposes, the 'L-code' has to be used to order the right colour at a paint shop. This L-code also appears on the sticker fixed on the metal partition

Regular paint codes 1968–73

Plate code	Colour (German) Body	Roof	Colour (English) Body	Roof	L-code Body	Roof	Years
0101	Orientblau	–	Orient Blue	–	L53H	–	1973
0106	Orientblau	Pastellweiß	Orient Blue	Pastel White	L53H	L90D	1973
0202	Savannenbeige	–	Savanna Beige	–	L620	–	1968–70
0206	Kasanrot	–	Kasan Red	–	L30B	–	1973
0261	Savannenbeige	Wolkenweiß	Savanna Beige	Cloud White	L620	L581	1968–70
0303	Chiantirot	–	Chianti Red	–	L31H	–	1971–72
0306	Chiantirot	Pastellweiß	Chianti Red	Pastel White	L31H	L90D	1971–72
0310	Chiantirot	Schwarz	Chianti Red	Black	L31H	L041	1971
0404	Sierragelb	–	Sierra Yellow	–	L11H	–	1971–72
0406	Sierragelb	Pastellweiß	Sierra Yellow	Pastel White	L11H	L90D	1971–72
0410	Sierragelb	Schwarz	Sierra Yellow	Black	L11H	L041	1971
0505	Niagarablau	–	Niagara Blue	–	L53D	–	1971–72
0506	Niagarablau	Pastellweiß	Niagara Blue	Pastel White	L53D	L90D	1971–72
0510	Niagarablau	Schwarz	Niagara Blue	Black	L53D	L041	1971
0606	Pastellweiß	–	Pastel White	–	L90D	–	1971–73
0610	Pastellweiß	Schwarz	Pastel White	Black	L90D	L041	1971
0706	Leuchtorange	Pastellweiß	Brilliant Orange	Pastel White	L20B	L90D	1973
0707	Leuchtorange	–	Brilliant Orange	–	L20B	–	1973
0909	Ulmengrün	–	Elm Green	–	L60D	–	1971–72
0906	Ulmengrün	Pastellweiß	Elm Green	Pastel White	L60D	L90D	1971–72
0910	Ulmengrün	Schwarz	Elm Green	Black	L60D	L041	1971
1313	Perlweiß	–	Pearl White	–	L87	–	1968
1706	Sumatragrün	Pastellweiß	Sumatra Green	Pastel White	L61B	L90D	1973
1717	Sumatragrün	–	Sumatra Green	–	L61B	–	1973
2006	Ceylonbeige	Pastellweiß	Ceylon Beige	Pastel White	L13H	L90D	1973
2020	Ceylonbeige	–	Ceylon Beige	–	L13H	–	1973
2222	Deltagrün	–	Delta Green	–	L610	–	1969–70
2261	Deltagrün	Wolkenweiß	Delta Green	Cloud White	L610	L581	1969–70
3838	Samtgrün	–	Velvet Green	–	L512	–	1968–70
4141	Lichtgrau	–	Light Grey	–	L345	–	1968–73
4242	Lotosweiß	–	Lotus White	–	L282	–	1968–70
4343	Tizianrot	–	Titian Red	–	L555	–	1968
4361	Tizianrot	Wolkenweiß	Titian Red	Cloud White	L555	L581	1968
4646	Elfenbein	–	Ivory	–	L567	–	1968–73
4747	Neptunblau	–	Neptune Blue	–	L50K	–	1968–73
4761	Neptunblau	Wolkenweiß	Neptune Blue	Cloud White	L50K	L581	1968–70
4949	Grundiert	–	Primered	–	–	–	1968–73
6565	Kansasbeige	–	Kansas Beige	–	L91D	–	1971
6506	Kansasbeige	Pastellweiß	Kansas Beige	Pastel White	L91D	L90D	1971
6510	Kansasbeige	Schwarz	Kansas Beige	Black	L91D	L041	1971
6761	Brillantblau	Wolkenweiß	Brilliant Blue	Cloud White	L50H	L581	1970
6767	Brillantblau	–	Brilliant Blue	–	L50H	–	1969–70
6861	Montanarot	Wolkenweiß	Montana Red	Cloud White	L30H	L581	1969–70
6868	Montanarot	–	Montana Red	–	L30H	–	1969–70

behind the driver's seat (the passenger seat on RHD vehicles).

SPECIAL PAINT-JOB CODES

The list is split into two sections: the 1968–71 section shows the old system of codes and the 1972–79 section shows the new system. Both lists have a column for the VW paint codes (commonly known as 'L-codes') as well as the paint codes in the international RAL standard. Most companies chose an RAL colour as their company colour, allowing for the possibility of ordering from different car manufacturers. The RAL standard covers a limited number of colours and not every colour can be translated into an RAL code. Where an RAL code does not exist, a blank space has been left.

Regular paint codes 1973–79

Plate code	Colour (German) Body	Roof	Colour (English) Body	Roof	L-code Body	Roof	Years	Remarks
4803	Agatabraun	Atlasweiß	Agate Brown	Atlas White	L86Z	L91Z	1977	Champagne Ed. I (S723)
4817	Dattelbraun	Fuchsrot	Date Brown	Fox Red	LH8A	LH3A	1978	Champagne Ed. II (S765)
4831	Agatabraun	Pastellweiß	Agata Brown	Pastel White	L86Z	L90D	1978	Westfalia Campmobile Champagne Ed. II (S765)
4991	Silbermetallic	–	Silver Metallic	–	L97A	–	1978–79	Silberfisch (S766)
A7A7	Lichtgrau	–	Light Grey	–	L345	–	1974–79	
A9A9	Grundiert	–	Primered	–	–	–	1974–79	
B1B1	Baligelb	–	Bali Yellow	–	L62H	–	1974	
B9B9	Elfenbein	–	Ivory	–	L567	–	1974–79	
D1D1	Ceylonbeige	–	Ceylon Beige	–	L13H	–	1974	
D1R1	Ceylonbeige	Pastellweiß	Ceylon Beige	Pastel White	L13H	L90D	1974	
D5D5	Dakotabeige	–	Dakota Beige	–	L13A	–	1978	
D9D9	Mexicobeige	–	Mexico Beige	–	LE1M	–	1979	
E1E1	Leuchtorange	–	Brilliant Orange	–	L20B	–	1974–79	
E1R1	Leuchtorange	Pastellweiß	Brilliant Orange	Pastel White	L20B	L90D	1974–77	
E6E6	Marinogelb	–	Chrome Yellow	–	L20A	–	1976–77	To chassis no. 2172 079 871
	Marinogelb	–	Chrome Yellow	–	L21H	–	1977–79	From chassis no. 2172 079 872 and up
E6R1	Marinogelb	Pastellweiß	Chrome Yellow	Pastel White	L20A	L90D	1976–77	
E9D9	Panamabraun	Mexicobeige	Panama Brown	Mexico Beige	L12A	LE1M	1979	
G1G1	Kasanrot	–	Kasan Red	–	L30B	–	1974–75	
G1R1	Kasanrot	Pastellweiß	Kasan Red	Pastel White	L30B	L90D	1974–75	
G9G9	Senegalrot	–	Senegal Red	–	L31A	–	1976–79	
G9R1	Senegalrot	Pastellweiß	Senegal Red	Pastel White	L31A	L90D	1976–79	
J2J2	Orientblau	–	Orient Blue	–	L53H	–	1974–75	
J2R1	Orientblau	Pastellweiß	Orient Blue	Pastel White	L53H	L90D	1974–75	
J4J4	Ozeanicblau	–	Reef Blue	–	L57H	–	1976–79	
J4R1	Ozeanicblau	Pastellweiß	Reef Blue	Pastel White	L57H	L90D	1976–79	
J6J6	Neptunblau	–	Neptune Blue	–	L50K	–	1974–79	
M4M4	Sumatragrün	–	Sumatra Green	–	L61B	–	1974–75	
M4R1	Sumatragrün	Pastellweiß	Sumatra Green	Pastel White	L61B	L90D	1974–75	
P4D9	Taigagrün	Mexicobeige	Sage Green	Mexico Beige	L63H	LE1M	1979	
P4P4	Taigagrün	–	Sage Green	–	L63H	–	1976–79	
P4R1	Taigagrün	Pastellweiß	Sage Green	Pastel White	L63H	L90D	1976–79	
R1R1	Pastellweiß	–	Pastel White	–	L90D	–	1974–79	
T1D5	Agatabraun	Dakotabeige	Agate Brown	Dakota Beige	L86Z	L13A	1978	
T1D9	Agatabraun	Mexicobeige	Agate Brown	Mexico Beige	L86Z	LE1M	1979	

paint and interior colours

Plate	code	German name	English name	L-code	RAL-code	Remarks
521	...					
522	...					
523	...					
524	...					
526	...					
	006	Ebenholzschwarz/Lotosweiß	Ebony Black/Lotus White	L041/L282	–	Taxi
	109	Gelb	Yellow	L263	1004	
	112	Gelb	Yellow	L262	1012	
	115	Elfenbein	Ivory	L567	1014	
	152	Chromgelb	Chrome Yellow	L16Q	1007	
	162	Gelb	Yellow	L11M	1006	
	169	Gelb	Yellow	L13R	1021	
	172	Gelb	Yellow	L14R	1011	
	173	Gelb	Yellow	–	1010	
	184	Sierragelb	Sierra Yellow	L11H	–	Westfalia
	200	Orange	Orange	L391	2000	Roadwork vehicles
	211	Signalorange	Signal Orange	L21M	2002	
	212	Orange	Orange	–	Mix of RAL 2002/2004	Siemens
	300	Feuerwehrrot	Fire Brigade Red	L256	3000	Fire Brigade vehicles
	306	Mittelrot	Middle Red	L054	3002	
	316	Rubinrot	Ruby Red	L456	–	
	326	AEG-Rot/AEG-Elfenbein	AEG-Red/AEG-Ivory	L256/L07Q	3000/1015	AEG
	329	Tizianrot	Titian Red	L555	–	
	331	Montanarot	Montana Red	L30H	–	Westfalia
	337	Chiantirot	Chianti Red	L31H	–	Westfalia
	508	Blau	Blue	L239	5010	Interrent
	551	Neptunblau	Neptune Blue	L50K	–	Westfalia
	562	Brillantblau	Brilliant Blue	L50H	–	Westfalia
	570	Niagarablau	Niagara Blue	L53D	–	Westfalia
	614	Polizeigrün	Police Green	L217	6009	Police, Germany
	642	Samtgrün	Velvet Green	L512	–	Westfalia
	672	Deltagrün	Delta Green	L610	–	Westfalia
	683	Siemensgrün	Siemens Green	L69Q	–	Constructa
	694	Ulmengrün	Elm Green	L60D	–	Westfalia
	703	Lichtgrau	Light Grey	L345	–	Westfalia
	706	Grau	Grey	L028	7005	
	713	Grau	Grey	–	7021	
	806	Savannenbeige	Savanna Beige	L620	–	Westfalia
	811	Kansasbeige	Kansas Beige	L91D	–	Westfalia
	902	Emailleweiß	Enamel White	–	–	Margarine Union
	904	Polizeiweiß	Police White	L280		Police, Germany
	907	Perlweiß	Pearl White	L87	–	Westfalia
	910	Weiß	White	L089	9001	
	917	Lotosweiß	Lotus White	L282	–	Westfalia
	920	Perlweiß	Pearl White	L87	–	Westfalia
	926	Pastellweiß	Pastel White	L90D	–	Westfalia

Plate code	German name	English name	L-code	RAL-code	Remarks
9002..	Ebenholzschwarz	Ebony Black	L041	–	
9005..	Gelb/Ebenholzschwarz	Yellow/Ebony Black	L263/L041	–	Jacobs, Bremen
9006..	Schwarz, *Dach und Stoßstangen* Weiß	Black, roof and bumpers White	L041/L282		Taxi
9020..	Papyrusweiß	Papyrus White	L90R	9018	
9104..	Rallyegelb	Rally Yellow	L10A	–	

Plate code	German name	English name	L-code	RAL-code	Remarks
9109..	Gelb	Yellow	L263	1004	
9110..	Gelb/Ebenholzschwarz	Yellow/Ebony Black	L15R/L041	1018/–	Firma Schindler
9112..	Gelb	Yellow	L262	1012	
9115..	Elfenbein	Ivory	L567	1014	Like Ambulance
9117..	Wagner-Gelb	Wagner Yellow	L17M	–	Reifen-Wagner
9121..	Sonnengelb	Sun Yellow	L13K	–	
9129..	Gelb	Yellow	L13R	1021	Veith-Pirelli
9130..	Lichtgelb	Bright Yellow	L367	1000	Alpenmilch
9131..	Kärcher-Gelb	Kärcher Yellow	L17N	Kärcher	
9134..	ADAC-Gelb	ADAC Yellow	L565	ADAC	
9139..	Lufthansa-Gelb	Lufthansa Yellow	L664	–	Lufthansa
9146..	Currygelb	Curry Yellow	L13N	1027	
9147..	Gelb	Yellow	L14N	1002	
9148..	Saharagelb	Sahara Yellow	L10P	1001	
9151..	Colarot-Neu/Papyrusweiß	Cola Red-New/Papyrus White	L35Q/L91Q	–/9010	Coca-Cola
9152..	Chromgelb *Radkappen und Stoßstangen* Chromgelb	Chrome Yellow, Hubcaps and bumpers Chrome Yellow	L16Q	1007	Not the same colour as L20A or L21H!
9156..	Marinogelb	Chrome Yellow	L20A	–	To VIN 2x72 079 871. Westfalia
9156..	Marinogelb	Chrome Yellow	L21H	–	From VIN 2x72 079 872 and up. Westfalia
9157..	Marinogelb, *Dach* Pastellweiß	Chrome Yellow, roof Pastel White	L20A/L90D	–	To VIN 2x72 079 871. Westfalia
9157..	Marinogelb, *Dach* Pastellweiß	Chrome Yellow, roof Pastel White	L21H/L90D	–	From VIN 2x72 079 872 and up. Westfalia
9162..	Gelb	Yellow	L11M	1006	
9164..	Hannen-Gelb	Hannen Yellow	L11R	–	Hannen Brauerei
9169..	Gelb	Yellow	L13R	1021	Monarch Firm/BP-Hamburg
9170..	Gelb	Yellow	L11P	1005	
9172..	Gelb	Yellow	L14R	1011	Edeka
9173..	Gelb	Yellow	L15R	1018	Shell
9175..	Saturngelb	Saturn Yellow	L13M	1016	
9179..	Gelb-Braun/Weiß	Yellow-Brown/White	L17R/L088	–	Bahlsen
9180..	Chromgelb, *Radkappen und Stoßstangen* Serie	Chrome Yellow, hubcaps and bumpers standard colour	L16Q	1007	Demag
9184..	Sierragelb	Sierra Yellow	L11H	–	Westfalia
9188..	Sierragelb	Sierra Yellow	L11H	–	
9191..	Elfenbein	Ivory	L07Q	1015	Taxi
9194..	Gelb/Blau	Yellow/Blue	L12H/L59Q	1017/5015	Blase, Lübecke
9195..	Gelb	Yellow	L263	1004	Hertz
9198..	Schindler-Gelb/Ebenholzschwarz	Schindler Yellow/Ebony Black	L14M/L041	–	Schindler
9200..	Orange	Orange	L591	2000	Roadwork Vehicles
9203..	Wüstenrot-Orange	Wüstenrot Orange	L26N	–	Wüstenrot
9211..	Orange	Orange	L21M	2002	
9212..	Orangerot	Orange-Red	L23Q	–	Siemens
9214..	Orange	Orange	L24Q	2001	
9221..	Orange, *Radkappen und Stoßstangen* Orange	Orange, hubcaps and bumpers Orange	L26Q	2004	Flughafen AG, Frankfurt am Main
9222..	Braun-Orange	Brown-Orange	L20P	–	Klöckner & Co., Duisburg
9224..	Orange, *Räder, Radkappen und Stoßstangen* Ebenholzschwarz	Orange wheels, hubcaps and bumpers Ebony Black	L26Q/L041	2004/-	Katastrophenschutz, Germany
9225..	Orange/Weiß	Orange/White	L27Q/L088	2003/1013	Firma Seba Dynatronic
9226..	Leuchtorange	Brilliant Orange	L20B	–	Westfalia
9227..	Leuchtorange, *Dach* Pastellweiß	Brilliant Orange, roof Pastel White	L20B/L90D	–	Westfalia
9232..	Orange	Orange	L27Q	2003	
9300..	Feuerwehrrot	Fire Brigade Red	L256	3000	Fire Brigades

(continued overleaf)

Plate code	German name	English name	L-code	RAL-code	Remarks
9302..	Feuerrot	Fire Red	L256	3000	Daimon
9303..	Feuerrot	Fire Red	L256	3000	
9306..	Mittelrot	Middle Red	L054	3002	
9310..	Burgunderrot	Burgundy Red	L095	–	Hastra
9311..	Kasanrot/Pastellweiß	Kasan Red/Pastel White	L30B/L90D	–	
9313..	Signalrot	Signal Red	L550	RAL-key 3	Fire Brigades, Austria
9314..	Miele-Rot	Miele Red	L551	–	Miele
9315..	Colarot-Neu	Cola Red-New	L35Q	–	Coca-Cola
9318..	Leuchtrot	Brilliant Red	L30Z	3024	Fire Brigades
9323..	Rot	Red	L39Q	3005	Hastra
9324..	Altrosa	Dusky Pink	L33X	3014	
9326..	Feuerrot/Weiß	Fire Red/White	L256/L088	3000/1013	AEG
9327..	Marsrot	Mars Red	L31B	–	
9330..	Montanarot	Montana Red	L30H	–	
9337..	Senegalrot	Senegal Red	L31A	–	
9350..	Chiantirot	Chianti Red	L31H	–	
9351..	Kasanrot	Kasan Red	L30B	–	
9353..	Phoenixrot	Phoenix Red	L32K	–	
9451..	Taigagrün	Sage Green	L63H	–	Westfalia
9452..	Taigagrün, *Dach* Pastellweiß	Sage Green, roof Pastel White	L63H/L90D	–	Westfalia
9453..	Sumatragrün/Pastellweiß	Sumatra Green/Pastel White	L61B/L90D	–	
9454..	Sumatragrün	Sumatra Green	L61B	–	
9461..	Grün	Green	L46M	6010	
9508..	Blau	Blue	L239	5010	Interrent
9511..	Blau	Blue	L433	5003	
9513..	Miamiblau	Miami Blue	L51C	–	
9514..	Blau	Blue	L536	5007	
9516..	Linnenblau	Linen Blue	L534	5011	
9518..	Grünblau	Green-Blue	L55P	5001	
9519..	Orientblau/Pastellweiß	Orient Blue/Pastel White	L534H/L90D	–	
9520..	Königsblau	Kings Blue	L531	5002	Technisches Hilfswerk (THW), Germany
9523..	Karstadt-Blau	Karstadt Blue	L537	–	
9524..	Ozeanicblau	Reef Blue	L57H	–	
9535..	Beatblau	Beat Blue	L51M	–	
9540..	VW-Blau	VW-Blue	L633	–	
9541..	Islandblau	Island Blue	L641	–	Mühlens, Köln
9547..	Blau	Blue	L53Q	5013	
9548..	Linnenblau, *Dach*: Weiß	Linen Blue, roof: White	L534/-	5011/-	Police, The Netherlands
9550..	Lindeblau/Papyrusweiß	Linde Blue/Papyrus White	L54Q/L91Q	–/9010	
9551..	Neptunblau	Neptune Blue	L50K	–	
9553..	Hellblau	Light Blue	L535	5012	BBC, Mannheim and Quelle, Fürth
9554..	Conti-Blau	Conti Blue	L56Q	–	
9555..	Zenitblau	Zenit Blue	L639	–	
9560..	Brillantblau	Brilliant Blue	L50H	–	
9567..	Cobaltblau	Cobalt Blue	L630	–	
9570..	Niagarablau	Niagara Blue	L53D	–	Westfalia
9576..	Niagarablau	Niagara Blue	L53D	–	
9579..	Blau/Grau	Blue/Grey	L239/L77Q	5010/7033	Deutsche Philips
9587..	Marinablau	Marina Blue	L54D	–	
9588..	Enzianblau	Gentian Blue	L51B	–	
9590..	Blau	Blue	L59Q	5015	Klöckner-Humboldt-Deutz
9593..	Blau	Blue	L53P	5000	
9597..	Orientblau	Orient Blue	L53H	–	
9598..	Blau	Blue	L54P	–	
9603..	Sumatragrün, *Dach* Pastellweiß	Sumatra Green, roof Pastel White	L61B/L90D	–	Westfalia

Plate code	German name	English name	L-code	RAL-code	Remarks
9607..	Aero-Grün	Aero-Green	L69R	–	Flughafen AG
9609..	Olivgrün	Olive Green	L319	6014	Army, The Netherlands
9610..	Olivgrün	Olive Green	L319	6014	Army, Germany
9612..	Olivgrün	Olive Green	–	–	Army, The Netherlands, Switzerland
9614..	Grün	Green	L217	6009	
9619	Grün	Green	L67H	–	Deutsche Raiffeisen Warenzentrale
9620..	Hippie-Grün	Hippie Green	L63M	–	
9624..	Grün	Green	L64P	6018	Flughafen AG, Frankfurt am Main
9631..	Wiesengrün, *Räder und Stoßstangen* Rallyeschwarz, *Radkappen* Wiesengrün	Meadow Green, wheels and bumpers Rally Black, hubcaps Meadow Green	L489	6001	Stadtverwaltung Essen
9642..	Samtgrün	Velvet Green	L512	–	
9644..	Vaillant-Grün/Papyrusweiß	Vaillant Green/Papyrus White	L62N/L91Q	–/9010	Vaillant
9645..	Minzgrün	Mint Green	L66Z	6029	Police, Germany
9648..	Ravennagrün	Ravenna Green	L65K	–	Westfalia
9650..	Türkisblau	Turquoise Blue	L640	–	MHZ Hachtel & Co.
9651..	Flamuco-Grün	Flamuco Green	L65M	–	Flamuco, Frankfurt am Main
9652..	Brillantgrün	Brilliant Green	L614	6004	Stadtwerke Düsseldorf
9654..	Cliffgrün	Cliff Green	L61A	–	
9658..	Wiesengrün, *Räder, Radkappen, Stoßstangen* Serie	Meadow Green, wheels, hubcaps and bumpers standard colour	L489	6001	Deutsche Raifeisen Warenzentrale
9676..	Industriegrün	Industry Green	L67Q	6011	
9679..	Deltagrün	Delta Green	L610	–	
9682..	Dunkelgrün	Dark Green	L68Q	6005	
9683..	Siemens-Grün	Siemens Green	L69Q	–	Siemens Constructa
9689..	Samtgrün/Blauweiß	Velvet Green/Blue White	L512/L289	–	Neff, Frankfurt am Main
9690..	Grün	Green	L61R	6017	
9691..	Popgrün	Pop Green	L62M	–	
9694..	Ulmengrün	Elm Green	L60D	–	
9696..	BP Gelb-Weiß-Grün	BP Yellow-White-Green	L12P/L97Q/ L65R	–	BP, Hamburg
9697..	Grün	Green	L66R	6000	
9702..	Grau	Grey	L75Q	7035	
9703..	Lichtgrau	Light Grey	L345	–	
9706..	Grau	Grey	L028	7005	
9711..	Silbergrau	Silver Grey	L70M	7001	
9714..	Hoechst-Grau	Hoechst-Grey	L71N	–	
9745..	Grau	Grey	L75Q	7035	GEG, Hamburg
9802..	Ceylonbeige/Pastelweiß	Ceylon Beige/Pastel White	L13H/L90D	–	
9809..	Savannenbeige	Savanna Beige	L620	–	
9816..	Wolf-Müller-Braun	Wolf-Müller-Brown	L80M	–	Wolf-Müller
9818..	Braun	Brown	L81Q	8017	
9819..	Kansasbeige	Kansas Beige	L91D		
9821..	Gelb/Braun	Yellow/Brown	L263/L81M	1004/8015	Rheinische Braunkohle AG
9822..	Braun	Brown	L577	8016	J.J. Darboven, Hamburg
9823..	Braun	Brown	L87Q	8000	
9824..	Ceylonbeige	Ceylon Beige	L13H	–	Westfalia
9826..	Dakotabeige	Dakota Beige	L13A	–	Westfalia
9827..	Ceylonbeige	Ceylon Beige	L13H	–	
9830..	Dakotabeige, *Dach*: Pastellweiß	Dakota Beige, roof: Pastel White	L13A/L90D	–	Westfalia
9832..	Mexicobeige	Mexico Beige	LE1M	–	Westfalia
9846..	Minzgrün	Mint Green	L66Z	6029	Police, Germany

(continued overleaf)

Special paint job codes 1972–79 (*Sonderlackierungen*) (continued)

Plate code	German name	English name	L-code	RAL-code	Remarks
9900..	Lotosweiß	Lotus White	L282	–	
9904..	Polizei-Weiß	Police-White	L280	–	Police, Germany
9908..	Weiß	White	L088	1013	Gervais, München
9909..	BP-Weiß	BP-White	L97Q	–	BP
9910..	Weiß	White	L089	9001	
9915..	Reinweiß	Pure White	L584	–	Schöller, Nürnberg
9919..	Papyrusweiß	Papyrus Wit	L91Q	9010	
9920..	Perlweiß	Pearl White	L87	–	
9926..	Pastellweiß	Pastel White	L90D	–	Westfalia
9928..	Klarweiß	Clear White	L96Q	–	Margarine Union
9937..	Weiß/Minzgrün	White/Mint Green	L93Z/L66Z	9001/6029	Police, Germany
9940..	Weiß/Grün	White/Green	L93Z/L67Z	9001/-	Bavarian Police, Germany
9950..	Silbermetallic	Silver Metallic	L96D	–	

Interior codes (do not apply for 1968–71 Buses with a *Sonderlackierung*)

Plate code	Colour (German)	Colour (English)	Material	Years	Remarks
....06	Alabaster (Grau)	Alabaster (Grey)	Cloth	1972–74	M53
....09	Campingrot	Camping Red	Cloth	1974–76	Westfalia Campmobiles
....33	Hellgrau/Mittelgrau	Light Grey/Medium Grey	Leatherette	1968–70	
....34	Hellsand/Khakibraun	Light Sand/Khaki Brown	Leatherette	1968–70	
	Campinggrüngelb	Camping Green Yellow	Cloth	1976–78	Westfalia Campmobiles
....35	Dunkelblau	Dark Blue	Leatherette	1968	
....36	Beige	Beige	Leatherette	1968	
....40	Schwarz	Black	Leatherette	1969–71	
....41	Indischrot	Indian Red	Leatherette	1968	
	Campinggrünrot	Camping Green Red	Cloth	1976–78	Westfalia Campmobiles
....45	Mittelgrau	Medium Grey	Leatherette	1968–71	Only Type 27 (Ambulance)
....46	Campingbraunbeige	Camping Brown Beige	Cloth	1978	Westfalia Campmobiles
....47	Galarot	Gala Red	Leatherette	1969–71	
....49	Campingrün	Camping Green	Cloth	1974–76	Westfalia Campmobiles
....50	Schwarz	Black	Leatherette	1972–78	
....51	Dunkelbeige	Dark Beige	Leatherette	1969–76	
....52	Alabaster (Grau)	Alabaster (Grey)	Leatherette	1971–78	
....53	Kork	Cork	Leatherette	1971–72	
....55	Lederbeige	Leather Beige	Leatherette	1973–75	
....60	Galarot	Gala Red	Leatherette	1972–74	
....61	Mittelgrau	Medium Grey	Leatherette	1973–78	Only Type 27 (Ambulance)
....77	Canyonbraun	Canyon Brown	Leatherette	1976–78	
....90	Canyonbraun	Canyon Brown	Cloth	1976–77	M106
....93	Alabaster (Grau)	Alabaster (Grey)	Cloth	1975	M53
....94	Lederbeige	Leather Beige	Cloth	1975	M53
....A5	Marine (Dunkelblau)	Marine (Dark Blue)	Cloth	1978–79	Silberfisch (S766)
....AL	Canyonbraun	Canyon Brown	Cloth	1979	
....EB	Campinggrüngelb	Camping Green Yellow	Cloth	1979	Westfalia Campmobiles
....EC	Campinggrünrot	Camping Green Red	Cloth	1979	Westfalia Campmobiles
....ED	Campingbraunbeige	Camping Brown Beige	Cloth	1979	Westfalia Campmobiles
....K2	Pergament (Beige-Grau)	Parchment (Beige Grey)	Cloth	1977	Champagne Ed. I (S723)
....M9	Schiefer	Slate	Leatherette	1975–76	2/'75 – 1/'76, Type 21 only
....N1	Wacholder (Grün)	Juniper (Green)	Leatherette	1975–76	6/'75 - 12/'75, Type 21 only
....N2	Lapisblau	Lapis Blue	Leatherette	1976	9/'75 –12/'75, Type 21 only
....N3	Bambus (Beige)	Bamboo (Beige)	Leatherette	1975	2/'75 – 6/'75, Type 23 only
....NM	Schwarz	Black	Leatherette	1979	
....NP	Canyonbraun	Canyon Brown	Leatherette	1979	
....NS	Alabaster	Alabaster (Grey)	Leatherette	1979	
....V1	Siena (Rot-Braun)	Sienna (Red Brown)	Cloth	1978	Champagne Ed. II (S765)

codes by destination

The M-plate of every Bay Window Bus gives exact information on the export destination. It can be read from the destination code, consisting of a combination of numbers or letters, or both. The numbers represent dealerships in West Germany that distributed the cars to other dealers in their area. In some cases, Buses were directly delivered to certain special customers, such as companies, organizations or authorities.

Until approximately chassis number 219 151 000 of model year 1969 there were no special codes for the German market. In these cases, the space for the destination code is left blank.

For some codes, the time periods within which they were used are shown.

The destination code 'Tourists' indicated that an overseas customer had picked up a Bus straight from the factory in Hannover. In the late 1960s and early 1970s this option was very popular with American and Canadian clients, who often used the opportunity to travel through Europe, before shipping their brand-new T2 back to their home country.

The 'Reserve' destination codes represent all the Buses that were not ordered by a particular client. Mostly, these Buses were used for presentations in VW Dealer showrooms.

GERMANY

Volkswagen Wholesale Dealers

NOTE: names of large dealerships in brackets.

17 March 1969 to 31 December 1975

001 = Aschaffenburg
002 = Baden-Baden
003 = Bad Kreuznach
004 = West-Berlin
006 = Bielefeld
007 = Bochum
008 = Braunschweig
009 = Bremen
010 = Darmstadt
011 = Dortmund
012 = Essen
013 = Ehingen
014 = Elmshorn
015 = Essen
016 = Frankfurt am Main
017 = Freiburg
018 = Friedberg
019 = Fulda
020 = Gießen
022 = Hagen (Röttger)
023 = Hamburg (Raffay)
024 = Hannover (Bischoff)
025 = Hildesheim
026 = Kaiserslautern
027 = Karlsruhe

028 = Kassel
029 = Kempten
030 = Kiel
031 = Koblenz
032 = Köln
033 = Lage
034 = Landshut
035 = Lübeck
036 = Lüneburg
037 = Mainz
038 = Mannheim
039 = Marburg
040 = Minden
041 = München (MAHAG)
042 = Münster
043 = Neheim-Hüsten
044 = Nienburg
045 = Nürnberg
046 = Offenburg
047 = Osnabrück
048 = Osterode
049 = Paderborn
050 = Passau
051 = Pforzheim
052 = Ravensburg
053 = Regensburg
054 = Reutlingen
055 = Siegen (Knebel)
056 = Singen
057 = Soest
058 = Stade
059 = Stuttgart

060 = Trier
061 = Tuttlingen
062 = Uelzen
063 = Wiesbaden
064 = Wolfsburg
065 = Würzburg
066 = Fürth
067 = Saarbrücken
068 = Augsburg
069 = Oldenburg
070 = Düsseldorf (Häberli)
071 = Recklinghausen
072 = Moers
073 = Duisburg
074 = Leverkusen
075 = Lehrte
076 = Wunsdorf
077 = Worms
078 = Neu-Ulm
079 = Memmingen
080 = Ansbach
081 = Hof
082 = Göttingen
083 = Heilbronn
084 = Ulm
085 = Krefeld
086 = Aurich
101 = Hamburg (Junge)
102 = Hamburg (Wiegmann)
103 = Hamburg-Harburg (Südekum)
104 = Hamburg-Altona (Köster)
105 = Hannover-Linden (Gessner)
106 = Hannover (Müller)

Distribution Centres

1st of January 1976 onwards

121 = VW-Audi Vertriebszentrum
    Schleswig-Holstein, Kiel
122 = VW-Audi Vertriebszentrum Weser-Ems,
    Bremen
123 = VW-Audi Vertriebszentrum Groß
    Hamburg, Hamburg
124 = VW-Audi-Vertrieb Nord-Niedersachsen,
    Wedemark
125 = VW-Audi Vertriebszentrum Südost
    Niedersachsen, Braunschweig
126 = VW-und Audi Vertrieb Nord-West,
    Münster
127 = VW-Audi Vertriebszentrum
    Ostwestfalen-Lippe, Lage

128 = VW-Audi Vertriebszentrum
    Nordhessen-Südniedersachsen, Kassel
131 = VW-Audi Vertriebszentrum Mittelrhein,
    Euskirchen-Kuchenheim
132 = VW-Audi-Vertriebszentrum Köln, Köln
133 = VW-Audi-Vertriebszentrum Rhein-Ruhr,
    Ratingen-Lintorf
134 = VW-Audi-Vertriebszentrum Westfalen,
    Unna
135 = VW-Audi Vertriebszentrum Saar-Pfalz,
    Kaiserslautern
136 = VW-Audi Vertriebszentrum Nord-
    Württemberg, Ludwigsburg-Nord
137 = VW-Audi Vertriebszentrum Südbaden,
    Freiburg
141 = V.A.G Vertriebszentrum Südbayern,
    München
142 = VW-Audi-Vertriebszentrum
    Rhein-Main, Frankfurt
143 = VW-Audi-Vertrieb Main-Fulda,
    Würzburg
145 = VW-Audi-Vertriebszentrum
    Bayern-Nord, Nürnberg
146 = VW-Audi-Vertrieb Berlin, West-Berlin

OTHER CODES

Major Customers,
Internal Destinations

888 No specific destination
901 Direct deliveries
902 Emergency car (police)
903 Bundespost (German Mail)
904 Bundesbahn (German Railroads)
905 VW employees
906 Bundeswehr (German Army)
907 Fire brigades
908 Bundesinnenministerium (Federal
    Ministry of the Interior)
909 Deployment forces
910 Fleet of cars VW AG
911 Leasing
912 Depositors
913 Diplomats
914 Daug
915 Porsche Vertriebsgesellschaft
916 Post
917 Bundesgesundheitsministerium
    (Federal Ministry of Health)
918 VW staff cars group 1,2,3
919 Bayerisches Rotes Kreuz
    (Bavarian Red Cross)
920 Vehicles for the press
921 Bundesfinanzministerium
    (Federal Ministry of Finance)
922 0-series cars
923 Staff cars AUDI NSU
925 Westfalia-Werke, Wiedenbrück
927 Kfz Park

928 Karmann Mobil
929 Karosseriewerke Weinsberg

World Export Destinations

A

AA = Afghanistan
AC = Australia CKD
AD = Australia, Brisbane
AE = Australia, Adelaide
AF = Australia, Freemantle
AG = Egypt VW
AJ = Angola, Luanda
AK = Djibouti
AL = Algeria
AM = CKD-steering American engines
AO = Angola, Lobito
AR = Argentina
AS = Australia, Melbourne
AZ = Albania

B

BA = Peoples Republic of South Yemen
BB = Bahrain
BD = Burundi
BE = Belgium
BF = Bahamas, Freeport
BG = Bulgaria
BH = Bahrain
BN = British New Guinea
BO = Bolivia
BR = Brazil
BS = British Solomon Islands
BU = Burma
BW = British Samoa
BX = Belgium (reserve)
BZ = Bangladesh

C

CA = Ecuador, Induauto VWI, VW
CC = Ecuador, Ambato VWI, VW
CF = Ecuador, Vaca VWI, VW

D

DA = Denmark, Copenhagen
DD = German Democratic Republic
DO = Denmark, Odense
DR = Denmark (reserve)
DU = United Arab Emirates, Dubai
DV = direct sales Porsche

E

EA = Zaïre, Kisangani
EB = United Kingdom, Belfast
EC = Peoples Republic of China
ED = Zaïre, Lubumbashi
EE = Sri Lanka
EG = United Kingdom, Grimsby
EH = Chile
EL = England, Leith
EM= Zaïre, Kananga
EN = United Kingdom, Ramsgate
EO = Ecuador, Ambato
EP = United Kingdom, Ramsgate (tourists)
ER = Ethiopia, Eritrea
ES = Czechoslovakia
ET = Zaïre, Kinshasa
EU = United Kingdom (reserve)
EY = Cyprus

F

FA = Ivory Coast, Abidjan
FB = Gabon, Libreville
FD = Cameroon
FF = Finland (reserve)
FG = Gabon, Port Gentil
FJ = Finland
FK = Senegal, Dakar
FL = Togo, Lome
FM = Mauritania
FN = Congo, Pointe-Noire
FO = People's Republic of Benin
FR = France
FT = Chad (Dewa W)
FU = France (reserve)
FV = Upper Volta
FW = Central African Republic
FX = France, Lyon
FY = Niger
FZ = Fiji Islands

G

GA = Gambia
GG = Ghana CKD
GH = Ghana
GJ = Gibraltar
GM = Guam
GR = Greece
GS = Greece, Saloniki
GZ = Gaza

H

HG = Hong Kong
HO = The Netherlands
HU = The Netherlands (reserve)

J

JB = Italy, Bologna
JC = Italy, Carimate
JD = Indonesia, Jayapura
JE = Indonesia, Massaua

JF = India, New Delhi
JG = Japan, Nagoya
JH = Indonesia, Makassar
JJ = India, Calcutta
JK = Iraq
JL = Israel
JM = Somalia
JN = Iran
JO = Jordan
JR = Republic of Ireland
JS = Iceland
JT = Indonesia, Surabaya
JU = Yugoslavia SKD
JV = Italy, Verona
JW = Indonesia, Medan-Belawan-Deli
JY = Japan, Yokohama
JZ = India, Panjim

K

KB = Cambodia
KE = Kenya
KF = Guinea-Bissau
KJ = Canary Islands, Las Palmas
KK = North Korea
KL = Kenya CKD Leyland
KN = Canada, St Johns N.B.
KP = Capeverdian Islands
KR = South Korea
KT = Canary Islands, Tenerife
KU = Kuwait
KX = Canada (tourists)

L

LA = Libya, Tripoli-Misurata
LB = Libya, Benghazi
LD = Libya, Benghazi-Derna
LE = Libya, Benghazi-Derna
LJ = Lebanon
LL = Liberia, Lower Buchanan
LM = Liberia, Monrovia
LN = Liberia, Monrovia
LO = Liberia, Tripoli-Oasis
LS = Liberia, Tripoli-Sebah
LU = Luxemburg
LY = Libya, Tripoli
LZ = Libya, Tripoli-Zuahara

M

MA = Malta
MB = Mozambique, Beira

MD = Madagascar
ME = Mexico
MF = Singapore, Brunei
MK = Morocco, Casablanca
ML = Malaysia, Kuala Lumpur
MM = Singapore
MO = Mozambique, Maputo
MS = Mauritius
MU = Mexico (reserve)
MW = Malawi
MZ = Mali

N

NC = Nigeria (VW of Nigeria)
NE = Nepal
NH = New Hebrides
NJ = Nigeria, Mandilas
NK = New Caledonia
NN = Norway (reserve)
NO = Norway
NS = New Zealand
NU = O-series

O

OA = Middle East GTZ
OB = Middle East UNO and sub-organizations
OC = Europe UNO and sub-organizations
OD = West Africa UNO and sub-organizations
OE = Europe GTZ
OF = West Africa GTZ
OG = Middle and South America UNO and
       sub-organizations
OH = North America UNO and sub-
       organizations
OJ = Middle East other special-organizations
OK = East Africa UNO and sub-organizations
OL = Middle and South America GTZ
OM = Oman, Muscat
ON = North America GTZ
OO = East America GTZ
OP = Far East GTZ
OQ = Europe other special organizations
OR = Austria, Salzburg
OS = Austria, Sparer
OU = Austria (reserve)
OW = Austria, Wien
OV = West Africa other special organizations
OX = Middle and South America other
       special organizations
OY = East Africa other special organizations
OZ = North America other special organizations

(MS).

P

PA = Panama
PC = Pakistan
PE = Peru
PG = Paraguay
PH = Philippines
PL = Poland
PN = Pakistan
PO = VW do Portugal
PP = test vehicle programme
PR = Puerto Rico
PS = VW Portugal CKD
PU = dispositions reserve export

Q

QA = Qatar and Abu Dhabi (U.A.E.)
QD = Qatar, Doha

R

RE = Réunion
RH = Rhodesia via Beira, Mozambique
RS = Rhodesia via Lourenço Marques
      (Maputo), Mozambique
RU = Romania
RW = Rwanda

S

SA = Saudi Arabia East, Damman
SC = Spanish Morocco, Ceuta
SD = Sweden-South
SE = Switzerland (reserve)
SF = South Africa
SH = Switzerland, Birfeld
SL = Sierra Leone
SM = Spanish Morocco, Melilla
SN = Sweden-North
SO = USSR
SQ = Syria (army)
SR = Sweden (reserve)
ST = Syria (Engineering & Automoti)
SU = Sudan
SV = Sweden-West
SW = Saudi Arabia West, Jeddah
SX = Saudi Arabia West, Damman
SY = Syria (Automaschine)
SZ = Switzerland

T

TE = Tourist Export Europe
TH = Thailand

TJ = Tahiti
TK = Turkey
TL = Thailand, Laos
TN = Tonga Islands
TO = São Tome
TR = USA (after-planning)
TS = Tanzania, Dar-Es-Salam
TU = Tunisia
TW = Taiwan
TX = Tourist Export Europe-West
TY = Canada (after-planning)

U

UA = USA, Los Angeles
UB = USA, Columbus via Baltimore
UC = USA, Chicago
UD = USA, Philadelphia/Baltimore
UE = USA (reserve after-planning)
UF = USA, San Francisco
UG = USA (after care)
UH = USA, San Antonio/Houston
UJ = USA, Jacksonville
UK = USA (reserve east)
UL = USA, St Louis/Lake Charles
UM = USA, Anchorage
UN = USA, New York
UO = USA, New Orleans
UP = USA, Portland via Seattle
UT = USA (tourist programme)
UU = USA, Los Angeles for Honolulu
UV = USA, Boston
UW = USA, Washington/Baltimore
UX = USA, Tourist Export-West
UY = USA, Grand Rapids/Toledo
UZ = USA (special care VWoA)

V

VG = Uganda
VJ = Vietnam
VN = Hungary
VR = Uruguay
VZ = Venezuela

W

WA = Antigua
WB = Netherlands Antilles, Aruba
WC = Bahamas
WD = Barbados
WE = Netherlands Antilles, Bonaire
WF = Costa Rica

(MS).

WG = Netherlands Antilles, Curaçao
WH = Dominica
WJ = Dominican Republic
WK = El Salvador (Autocar)
WL = El Salvador (Caribe-Motor)
WM = Grand Cayman
WN = Grenada
WO = Guadeloupe
WP = Guatemala
WQ = Guyana
WR = French Guyana
WS = Haiti
WT = British Honduras
WU = Honduras
WV = Jamaica
WW = Colombia
WX = Cuba
WY = Martinique
WZ = Montserrat

X

XB = Belgium
XD = Denmark, Copenhagen
XH = The Netherlands
XL = Luxemburg
XN = Norway
XO = Austria
XP = Spain, Cadiz

Y

YE = Yemen
YF = Finland
YJ = Iceland
YO = Yugoslavia, Sarajevo
YP = Spain, Irun
YZ = Yugoslavia, Zagreb (Kons)

Z

ZA = Nicaragua
ZB = Zambia, via Beira, Mozambique
ZC = Panama, Canal Zone
ZD = Panama
ZE = Puerto Rico
ZF = St Croix
ZG = St Kitts
ZH = St Lucia
ZJ = Ireland
ZK = Netherlands Antilles, St Maarten
ZL = St Martin
ZM = St Barthelemy
ZN = St Thomas Islands
ZO = St Vincent
ZP = Surinam
ZR = Trinidad
ZS = Costa Rica
ZT = Jamaica
ZU = Honduras
ZY = Tortola
ZV = Ecuador, Guayaquil
ZW = Ecuador, Quito-Cahaze

1986: Brazilian T2 product range.

10

transporters *assembled* *or built* overseas

CKD TRANSPORTER ASSEMBLY WORLDWIDE

The worldwide success of the Beetle and the T1 gave Volkswagen the perfect opportunity to conquer overseas markets with new products. Due to the high import taxes that were levied on luxury products, including cars, in many countries, VW introduced the CKD system, meaning 'completely knocked down'. Vehicles were shipped abroad in unfinished form in single parts and modular 'knocked-down' groups of parts in easily transportable packaging cases. The parts were packaged in a way that made assembly easy in the destination market.

The marketing department was particularly interested in extending sales of the new Bay Window Bus in Asia and Central America. VW decided to enlarge its CKD assembly to satisfy this demand for a cheap, light transport vehicle. In countries such as Indonesia, Thailand, the Philippines, Malaysia, Pakistan, Peru, Sri Lanka, Senegal, Finland, Turkey, Egypt, Ecuador, Ghana, Mexico and Kenya, special plants were opened and

equipped to do the assembly work. The table below shows all the locations with CKD companies that received parts from the Hannover factory in the 1970s.

The CKD programme was limited to simple models such as the Panelvans, Kombis and Pick-Ups. Luxury Transporters or special models were not part of the programme, since they were too expensive for the overseas markets and too complex to knock down and to reassemble.

CKD locations worldwide

Model	Country	Year of beginning	Year of ending
T2 Kombi/Pick-Up	Indonesia	1971	1978
T2 Kombi/Pick-Up	Thailand	1972	1975
T2 Panelvan	Philippines	1973	1976
T2 Panelvan	Indonesia	1974	1974
T2 Panelvan	Malaysia	1974	1974
T2 Panelvan	Pakistan	1974	1975
T2 Panelvan	Peru	1974	1977
T2 Panelvan	Thailand	1974	1974
T2 Panelvan	Sri Lanka	1974	1974
T2 Panelvan	Senegal	1974	1977
T2 Panelvan	Finland	1974	1975
T2 Panelvan	Turkey	1974	1976
T2 Panelvan	Egypt	1974	1976
T2 Panelvan	Ecuador	1974	1974
T2 Panelvan	Ghana	1975	1975
T2 Panelvan	Mexico	1975	1977
T2 Kombi/Pick-Up	Kenya	1976	1980
T2 Kombi/Pick-Up	Ghana	1976	1976

BRAZILIAN TRANSPORTERS

VW do Brazil (VWB) started producing the first-generation Transporter on 2 September 1957 in São Bernardo do Campo near São Paulo. CKD kits from Germany had been assembled in this factory since 1953. Half of the parts needed for the reassembly were made locally and produced by VWB itself, while the rest were imported from Germany. Buses built in Brazil were produced not only for the home market, but also for South America and Central America.

The 'real' Split Window Buses were produced up to 1975. In the same year, VWB started to manufacture the Bus with components of the T1 and the T2.

The driver's cabin was almost the same as the one on German Buses and these 'mixed' Bay Windows were built right up to 1997.

In 1981 VWB introduced a water-cooled 1600cc diesel engine with 50bhp, available only for the Panelvan and the Pick-Up, and in the same year the double-cab Pick-Up was also presented.

In 1982, new features were introduced to the Brazilian Bus, including a new steering wheel, familiar from the

Year	Buses produced
1966	100,000
1977	500,000
1995	1,000,000

German T3, safety belts, and disc brakes in the front. In 1985 the diesel engine and the double-cab Pick-Up were removed from the sales programme because of lack of demand. In 2000 the Pick-Up ran out.

In 1997 the 'new' Kombi was introduced, no longer using parts of the Split Screen Bus (T1) and with a look that was similar to that of the German T2b. Nevertheless, the Brazilian Kombi had some modifications, including a slightly raised roof, a new steering wheel, new rear-view mirrors and some other detail changes. It is available with two engines, one running on methanol, the other the well-known Type I engine, now with 58bhp.

1986: 'mixed' luxury Kombi.

Double-cab Pick-Up with diesel engine (AG).

1986: single cab Pick-Up with enlarged metal platform.

1986: bi-coloured double-cab Pick-Up.

1986: Panelvan with side doors.

2003: the actual Brazilian T2.

In the current Brazilian Volkswagen programme, all Transporter models are named 'Kombi'. Five models of the Bay Window Bus are still available today:

■ School Bus 'Kombi-Escolar';
■ Panelvan 'Kombi-Furgão';
■ Kombi 12-seater 'Kombi-Lotação';
■ Kombi 'Kombi-Standard';
■ Ambulance 'Kombi-Ambulance'.

The Brazilian Kombi can be ordered only in white (Branco Gacial, 8G8G), but every two months, one day's production is finished in silver. The VW Kombi has about 40 per cent of the light commercial vehicles market in Brazil, partly because of the very affordable price of 24,108 Brazilian Real (about 6,500 Euros). Most Kombis in Brazil are used as taxis.

São Bernado do Campo has been producing forty T2 Buses every day, and VWB plans to produce the T2 up to 2007. In November 2005 the aircooled engine of the T2 will be replaced by a watercooled one. However, the end of the T2's production era is coming closer. In comparison with newer Transporters, which have such features as ABS, airbag systems or catalytic converters, the T2 is starting to show its age. Technically, it cannot compete to satisfy the safety and environmental needs of drivers today.

MEXICAN TRANSPORTERS

VW de Mexico built the VW T2 for their home market from 1 October 1971 to 1996. Mexican Bay Window Buses were assembled in Puebla, one of the largest Volkswagen overseas production locations. (The Type I Beetle was also produced in Puebla, up to 2003.) Right from the start of the Mexican production, both the Kombi (or 'Combi', to give it its Mexican name) and the Panelvan ('Panel' to the Mexicans) were available.

During the production period of twenty-five years, some remarkable and visible changes to the drive element were developed for the Mexican T2. The Buses produced until 1987 ran with the well-known 1600cc air-cooled Type I engine, with 44bhp. In 1987 the T2 received a water-cooled inline engine from the VW Golf, with 71bhp. The front of the T2 had to be redesigned to accommodate the cooling, and it acquired a plastic grille and new plastic bumpers.

In 1991 the Mexican T2 also received a slightly raised roof, like its Brazilian brother, and in 1997 a new dashboard was fitted. From 1992 the Mexican Bay Window had been equipped with a fuel-injection installation instead of a carburettor, a catalytic converter, and an 85bhp engine.

In 1996, with an impressive number of about 250,000 Buses, production ended in Mexico. Bay Window Buses began to be imported from Brazil and then, in 2001, after thirty years, VW removed the T2 from its Mexican sales programme.

Brazil 2004: driver's cabin of actual T2 (AG).

Brazil 2004: engine from the bottom (AG).

Brazil 2004: engine from behind (AG).

ABOVE: *Brazil 2004: inside (AG).*
RIGHT: *Mexican T2 Kombi.*

Mexican T2 with the normal roof.

Mexican T2 with the new roof.

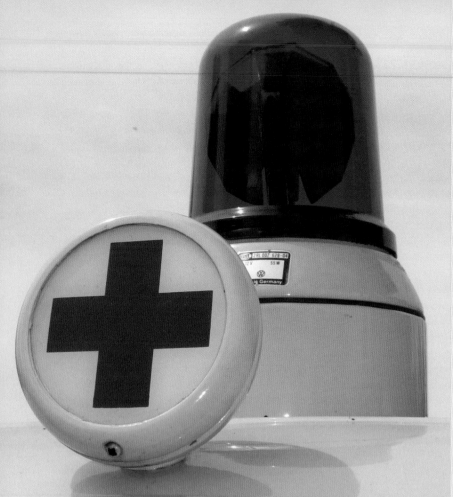

SO9, T2b (P).

SO9, T2a (APS).

11 special models

SO MODELS

Like its predecessor, the T2 was available not only as a standard production model, such as the Panelvan, the High-Roof Panelvan, the Pick-Up with single or double cab, the Kombi or the Microbus/Microbus L. Alongside these, special body conversions based on the Buses were custom-made for clients in trade and industry, as well as in local and state authorities. Some, such as Ambulances, Fire Trucks and Fire Brigade Commando Vehicles, were produced by VW itself. Models that required a lot of extra work, the so-called 'SO models' (as in *Sonderausführung*), were converted by specialized companies, including Westfalia, Meyer (Hagen), Auto Dunker (Friedberg) and Ruthmann. The SO models still had to be approved by the development department of the Volkswagenwerk, and they maintained a very high standard and the full ex-works warranty.

The VW conversion partners and their product ranges were as follows:

- Westfalia (Wiedenbrück): taxi, camper van, mobile office/police road traffic accident emergency vehicle, mobile shop, low-loader, pick-up with enlarged wooden platform;
- Meyer (Hagen): turntable ladder;
- Auto-Dunker (Friedberg)/Brown Boveri York (Mannheim): VW refrigerated vehicle;
- Anton Ruthmann (Gescher): hydraulic lifting platform;
- Autodienst Prometer (Lengerich): hydraulic tipper;
- Gebrüder Wolperdinger (Winsen/Luhe): pick-up with carrier for long pipes or poles;
- Fahrzeugfabrik Josef Fickers (Neuenhaus): pick-up with carrier for long pipes or poles

The *Sonderausführungen* could be ordered at any Volkswagen dealership, and were often defined by certain M-codes. Nevertheless, all these Buses were individually equipped with any approved M-code on the model type. The following list shows all available models with special SO numbers and the model year in which they were available.

SO3.

Outside (above) and inside (below) of the SO7.

SO Models

SO1	VW mobile shop	67–79
SO2	VW High-roof mobile shop	69–79
SO3	VW Kombi police road traffic accident emergency vehicle	67–79
SO5	VW Panelvan refrigerated vehicle with 140mm insulating board	67–79
SO6 II	VW Panelvan refrigerated vehicle with 80mm insulating board	67–79
SO6 III	VW Panelvan refrigerated vehicle with reinforced interior trim	67–79
SO6 III	VW Panelvan refrigerated vehicle for meat products (with aluminium trim and isolation)	68–79
SO6 IV	VW Panelvan refrigerated vehicle for meat products (with plastic material trim)	70–79
SO7	VW Panelvan refrigerated vehicle with chiller	67–79
SO8	VW Pick-Up hydraulic lifting platform (Ruthmann-Lifter, Type V 90)	67–79
SO9	VW Pick-Up hydraulic lifting platform (Ruthmann-Lifter, Type V 80)	67–79
SO10	VW Pick-Up hydraulic lifting platform (Ruthmann-Lifter, Type V 60)	67–79
SO11	VW Pick-Up turntable ladder	67–79
SO14	VW Pick-Up with carrier for long pipes or poles	67–79
SO15	VW Pick-Up hydraulic tipper	67–79
SO24	VW Pick-Up with trailer for longer pipes or poles	67–79
SO25	VW Pick-Up low-loader	67–79

SO15.

Interior of an SO5 Panelvan.

Identification plate of the converter.

Another form of special models were those that had initially been produced as standard model types and had been modified later by VW importers or external companies. These might include school buses, glass-sheet transporters, special Campmobiles, snow ploughs, Buses with workshop equipment, loudspeaker Kombis, stretched versions, air-traffic control vehicles, power unit heating panelvans, vegetable transporters, hearses, road sweepers, various types of fire truck, pick-ups with crane constructions on their platform, and prisoner or money transporters. The list goes on and on.

SO25: 1969 Low-Loader

One very rare model is the T2 Low-Loader indicated by the code M115 on the M-plate. It is rumoured that fewer than 200 of these vehicles were manufactured by Westfalia for Volkswagen.

The Bus shown here was built on 18 July 1969 on chassis number 260 2 120 055. It was ordered by VW itself (destination code 910), and probably used for exhibition purposes. In 1971, it was sold to the Malteser Hilfsdienst and it is now owned by a private collector in Germany.

M-Plate of the T2 Low-Loader

```
02 000 074

494951 029 115

29 5 7015 910 2610 11
```

T2a Low-Loader (APS).

Back of the Low-Loader with towing hook (APS).

With open gates and side-doors (APS).

Plane loading area; mounting for rotating light on the cabin (APS).

Side-door lock from inside (APS).

Enlarged bracket for the left side-view mirror (APS).

VW-Groentewagen

Technische gegevens

T2a vegetable transporter (P).

VW-Isolatiecontainer

Technische gegevens

T2a/b refrigerated vehicle (P).

VW-Isolatieopbouw

Technische gegevens

T2a/b refrigerated vehicle with big side doors (P).

VW-Glaswagen

Technische gegevens

T2a glass transporter (P).

T2b glass transporter (P).

VW-Ladderwagen

Technische gegevens

T2a/b ladder truck (P).

MAIN CONVERTERS

Pon's Automobielhandel

The programme of the Dutch importer Pon's Automobielhandel was remarkable for its wide range of useful T2 variations, including the following:

- T2 Pick-Up vegetable transporter: had a special construction for presenting and transporting vegetable crates. On the driver's side the body shell could be opened and closed with a tilt, so that the Bus could be used as a mobile vegetable shop;
- T2 Pick-Up refrigerated vehicle: had an isolated cooling shell construction for the transport of frosted food, very popular in the

Bedrijfswagennieuws
over de VW-LT: de grote bedrijfswagen van VW
Nummer 12 · 21 november 1975

Dustmaster op VW Kipper en VW-LT Kipper

T2b dustcart (P).

1970s. This conversion was available either with four side doors or with one enlarged door. Not available with panel lids;
- T2 Pick-Up glass transporter: a simple construction made out of steel and wood for the transport of large glass panes. The construction was easily removable, so that the

vehicle could be used as a normal Pick-Up;
- T2 Kombi ladder truck: a special ladder roof-rack was stowed in the back, and the ladder could be raised to a height of 10m and removed if the Bus has to fulfil other purposes;
- T2 Pick-Up tipmaster/dustmaster: had a hydraulic tippable refuse skip. The rear bumper had a piece cut out in the middle, so that the dust did not flip out while the skip was being unloaded. With two big flaps on every side of the body construction, the rubbish can be loaded easily. This conversion became very popular for borough and city councils because of its agility;
- T2 Pick-Up road sweeper: had a wooden platform and rotating brushes for street cleaning;

- T2 Pick-Up snow plough; had a hydraulic movable clearing shield;
- T2 Tipper.

Kemperink

Dutch manufacturer Kemperink was famous for its long-wheelbase T2 Buses. To achieve more space for the transport of light goods, Kemperink would take a standard or double-cab Pick-Up, strip it down totally and enlarge the whole structure and the chassis. The Dutch biscuit company Bolletje Beschuit had a large number of Kemperink Panelvans in its fleet, hence the Dutch nickname for the conversion – 'Bolletje Bus'.

The T2 was available in the following Kemperink conversions:

- T2 long-wheelbase extended box van;
- T2 long-wheelbase extended Pick-Up;
- T2 long-wheelbase extended double-cab Pick-Up;
- T2 Campmobiles.

Westfalia

Volkswagen offered the T2 Westfalia Campmobile right from the start of production. The vehicles were usually produced at the Hannover factory and then fitted out with special interior camping equipment, as well as the famous pop-up roof, at Westfalia in Wiedenbrück.

To identify the differences in the interior layout or equipment between the various models, every sort of Campmobile got its own SO-code. Some of them (the SO72, 73, 76 models) were named after European cities. The models of the first series were called 'Oslo', 'Stockholm', 'Amsterdam', 'Brussels', 'Paris', 'Zürich' and 'Rome'.

One very simple Camper was the SO36, a Kombi (Type 23) with a polyester elevating roof. SO models 60 to 62 and SO70 continued with the successful 'Mosaik' range, well known from the days of the T1. They were based on a T2 Kombi, but the entire interior in the passenger or cargo compartment could be removed, allowing the vehicle to be used flexibly, as a camper van, or as a normal Transporter or passenger carrier. The T2 with 'Mosaik' (later, 'Camping' equipment) was a real value-added Transporter.

T2a/b that can be used as road sweeper or snow-plough (P).

T2a tipper (P).

Kemperink: T2b long wheelbase extended Pick-Up.

Kemperink: T2b long wheelbase extended Boxvan.

ABOVE: *Kemperink: T2b long wheelbase extended double-cab Pick-Up.*

LEFT: *Manufacturer plate of Kemperink.*

SO61 Kombi with Westfalia-Kit (Mosaik).

Westfalia SO-codes for Campers

Code	Model	Years
SO36	VW-Kombi with polyester elevating roof	68–73
SO60	VW-Camper 60	68
SO61	VW-Camper-Mosaik (Kit 61)	68
SO62	VW-Camper 62	68
SO69/1	VW-Camper 'Oslo'	69–70
SO69/2	VW-Camper 'Zürich'	69–70
SO69/3	VW-Camper 'Stockholm'	69–70
SO69/4	VW-Camper 'Brüssel'	69–70
SO69/5	VW-Camper 'Paris'	69–70
SO69/6	VW-Camper 'Rome'	69–70
SO69/7	VW-Camper 'Amsterdam'	69–70
SO70/1	VW-Camper Kit SO70/1 'Mosaik'	69–70
SO72	VW-Camper	71–75
SO72/1	VW-Camper 'Luxemburg'	71–73
SO72/2	VW-Camper 'Los Angeles'	71–73
SO72/3	VW-Camper 'Helsinki'	71–73
SO72/4	VW-Camper 'Houston'	71–73
SO72/5	VW-Camper 'Madrid'	71–73
SO72/6	VW-Camper 'Miami'	71–73
SO72/7	VW-Camper 'Mosaik'	71–74
SO72/8	VW-Camper 'Mosaik'	71–74
SO72/9*	VW-Camper Kit 'Mosaik'	75–76
SO72/13	VW-Camper 'Continental' (RHD)	72–74
SO73/1	VW-Camper 'Düsseldorf'	74–75
SO73/2	VW-Camper 'Dallas' (USA)	74–75
SO73/3	VW-Camper 'Malaga'	74–75
SO73/4	VW-Camper (USA)	74–75
SO73/5	VW-Camper 'Offenbach'	74–75
SO73/6	VW-Camper (USA)	74–75
SO73/7	VW-Camper 'Helsinki'	75–79
SO73/11	VW-Camper 'Oxford' (RHD)	76–79
SO76/1	VW-Camper 'Berlin'	76–79

* from model year 1977 the kit was available without an SO number

Roof-rack of a T2a Camper.

SO36 (Westfalia).

The 100,000th Campmobile was produced at Westfalia on 23 June 1971. Around that time, about 60 per cent of the Campmobile production was ordered by the US market, so the importer, Volkswagen of America, decided to rename all the SO models after American cities.

From model year 1974, the Campers were equipped with a new big pop-up roof, a double bed and the luggage tub in the front.

Kitchen of a 1974 Camper.

T2a Westfalia Camper (1967).

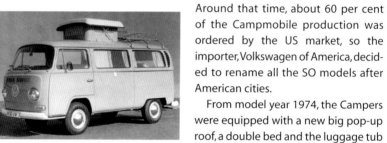

Interior of the 1974 Westfalia Camper.

Spare tyre box for European Westfalia Campers.

Lammella windows for the Camper (RR).

Inside the pop-up roof.
T2b Westfalia Camper (1974).

T2b Camper Karmann Mobil (MS).

Other Camping Conversion Firms

The enormous demand for camper vans at the beginning of the 1970s allowed a number of conversion firms to build a business in converting campers, including the following:

- Dormobile: British company well known for its T1 conversions, and famous for a special kind of pop-up roof (hinged at the side);
- Bischoffsberger: German VW dealer who introduced a very new form of Campmobile around 1975. A T2b Transporter was stripped down, leaving only chassis and cabin, then a large insulated body (Kranich) was built on, allowing camping holidays in very cold weather;
- Tischer: produced a removable camping body construction for the VW T2 Pick-Up, which could be attached to its platform for the holiday season, giving more flexibility;
- Karmann Mobil: up to the newest Transporter of the fifth generation and the LT2, Karmann Mobil was an official partner of Volkswagen, and their conversions can be ordered at

any German Volkswagen dealer. The company came out with a special conversion in 1977;
- Syro: German firm offering modularized camping parts for supplementary fitting in the VW Kombi, similar to Westfalia's 'Mosaik' concept.

CONVERSIONS

T2 Taxi

Volkswagen introduced the Type 241 311, named 'VW-Taxi/VW-Taxi L', in model year 1968. This T2 Taxi was a spacious passenger vehicle for the German market, built at the Westfalia factory in Wiedenbrück and based on a standard Type 22 or 24.

German law required taxis to be equipped in a certain way, so Volkswagen provided the following features on the Type 241 311 Taxi:

- paint colour: Ebony Black L41 (body) and Lotus White L282 (roof) (special paint instruction 52X006) from model year 1968 on; on 18.12.1970, the body colour was altered to Ivory L07Q (special paint instruction

9191) because of a change in German Taxi regulations;
- two sliding doors;
- steering lock;
- Eberspächer BN4 heater with outlet in passenger compartment;
- sliding door on left and right side;
- automatic step on passenger side (M420);
- foot-operated alarm installation (M533);
- speaker and microphone for communication between driver and passengers (M534);
- yellow 'Taxi' sign with black lettering;
- black sign with yellow lettering Frei ('Free') in the windscreen.

In 1968, a German law dictated that all taxis had to have a division between cabin and passenger compartment for safety reasons, but that the driver should still be able to see the client. Westfalia was not able to fulfil this demand, so Volkswagen went to Karosserie- und Fahrzeugwerke Wilhelm Thiele (Bremen), a company experienced in such conversions. A special division was built between cabin and passenger compartment, reinforced in the upper part with 27-mm bullet-proof glass, but the law was cancelled just one year later.

The following equipment was orderable for the VW T2 Taxi (Westfalia Taxi equipment codes for Type 241 311):

- Z4005 – dividing wall with partitioning glass and plate for paying;
- Z4006 – dividing wall with partitioning glass and without plate for paying;
- Z4007 – lockable link for foldable and arrestable backrest of the

T2 Taxi: Dividing wall with partitioning glass and without plate for paying (WT).

Armoured dividing wall (WT).

Front of a T2a Taxi (MS).

T2a Taxi in the streets of Hamburg (JW).

T2b Taxi.

two-seater bench (passenger compartment);
- Z4008 – lengthening of the heating pipe to heat the cabin;
- Z4009 – seat belts for the passenger compartment (three two-point safety belts and two three-point safety belts).

T2 Hearse

Not orderable as a regular SO model, the T2 hearse was a special redesign of the standard VW Panelvan. A good and solid T2 hearse conversion had been built by the German company Fritz Frickinger, located in Augsburg (Bavaria). These hearses were notable for their extremely large windows in the cargo compartment.

The hearse conversions were based on normal Panelvans, Pick-Ups or double-cab Pick-Ups, and were available right from the start of production of the T2, in 1967. These serial models were fitted out with a huge number of new body panels inside and outside, and could usually carry two coffins.

PANELVAN CONVERSION
Normally, the base model of the Panelvan had a black body colour, or was primered, and had a partitioning wall behind the driver's cabin. The sliding door was removed and a new outer body side quarter panel was welded in. The hearse conversion based on the

Panelvan was equipped with a raised floor, made of sheet metal, that was on a level with the floor area located over the rear engine. On top of the raised floor, a loading platform enabled easier handling of the coffins that had to be lifted in and out. An underfloor compartment door from the Pick-Up was set in, so that the space right underneath this second floor level could be used.

Inside walls, roof and rear flap were covered with plastic-laminated plywood. The floor covering was often made out of the same material, but was usually coated with blank sheet or aluminium plates.

Depending on the requirements of the individual customer and the country, the hearse had a large window with frosted or clear glass on each side.

PICK-UP/DOUBLE-CAB CONVERSION
Hearses built up on a Pick-Up and a double-cab version received a complete coachwork frame on the back, welded to the cabin and the loading platform. These conversions were often enlarged in the back, right behind the engine. The rear flap was enlarged, to give enough space to put in two coffins at the same time. One big advantage of the Hearse based on the double-cab version was that it could carry up to six persons. To make the T2 hearse into a vehicle more appropriate for its use, an aluminium ledge was fixed to both sides and the back of the Bus.

A small badge in the shape of a palm leaf was inserted as a frosted glass part into the side and back windows. In addition, some had a cross made out of steel on the front part of the roof.

VW CONVERSION
For the funeral procession of Heinz Heinrich Nordhoff, on 15 May 1968 in Wolfsburg (*see* page 7), the development department of Volkswagenwerk assembled a special hearse. Based on a T2a Pick-Up without a roof, the whole Bus, including the bumpers, was painted in Ebony Black.

This Pick-Up had some features originally known only on the Clipper, including mouldings on the front and rear bumper, the door and the front, a chromium-plated VW sign on the front, and whitewall tyres.

1968 AUSTRIAN HEARSE
This early, unique T2a Hearse, a conversion by the Adalbert Stadtherr KG company, of Wiener Neustadt (Austria), was based on a standard Panelvan. One of its most remarkable features was the large side windows.

The original sliding door got 'welded in', and the well for the sliding-door handle was removed. In the upper part, an underfloor compartment door, familiar on the single-cab Pick-Up model, was set in to use the space underneath the coffin. Inside, the cargo floor covering the engine was extended up to the metal partition of the cabin, building a second floor, which was covered in some kind of linoleum. A stretcher for one coffin was fixed on this construction.

This Panelvan had a number of unusual features, including the lack of any sort of top coat, having been painted with primer only. After the conversion, the Bus was painted black inside and outside, the bumpers were painted in silver. The leatherette interior was finished in the very rare colour beige, available in model year 1968 only.

The M-plate of this early Bay Window should be read like the M-plate of a T1. The top row shows the production date. The year of production can be identified by looking at the first digits of the chassis number in the last row on the right-hand side. This Panelvan was built on 21 March 1968 on chassis number 21 8 124 204, and left the factory to be delivered to Vienna (Austria).

Side view (above) and rear view (right) of the T2a/b Hearse converted by Frickinger (UM).

T2a Hearse VW conversion.

Wolfsburg: Heinrich-Nordhoff-Straße.

Arriving at the funeral hall.

Funeral march through Wolfsburg.

VW factory Wolfsburg 'Mittelstraße'.

VW factory Wolfsburg 'Mittelstraße'.

T2a Hearse 'Gemeinde und Sterbeverein Rohrbach b. M.'

Austrian hearse: inside the cargo compartment.

Austrian Hearse: original key with printed chassis number on aluminium plate.

In 2004 the current owner, the German Community of Interest T2, bought this hearse in Austria having run only 3,800km. The Panelvan is still equipped with its original motor, a 47 PS Type I engine with the early number B0 0840985.

M-Plate of the Austrian Hearse

21 3
510
11 030 043 092 500
OW 2110 494936 8124204

Fire Brigade Vehicles

As with the T1, the fire brigade vehicles based on the second generation were available right from the start of production, in 1967. The T2 was the most commonly used emergency vehicle of the German fire brigades, in the form of the 'classic' Fire Truck (Type 21F), Fire Brigade Crew Kombi and the Fire Brigade Commando vehicle. All were suitable for the job because of their robust and manoeuvrable body and an affordable price.

Apart from the standardized fire brigade vehicles, many Buses were built to special requirements in the Hannover service department of VW. Others were built by companies that specialized in producing fire-fighting vehicles.

VW Fire Truck

The best-selling 'small' fire engine in Germany was the Type 21F, available as a standard VW Fire Truck TSF (T) or as a VW Fire Truck with dry-powder extinguisher fittings. The name TSF (T) comes from the German *Tragkraft-Spritzen-Fahrzeug (Trupp)*, or 'mobile pump vehicle'. Based on the Type 21F, option M140 ('Fire truck to German specifications') had to be ordered.

Equipment features of the VW Fire Truck (Type 21F)

ABOVE LEFT: T2a/b Fire Truck Type 21F.

ABOVE: T2a/b with typical fire brigade equipment.

Exterior

- paint colour: body Fire Brigade Red L256 (RAL 3000); bumpers and wheels black (L41); from 1973 on, bumpers white (RAL 9010), wheels chrome-coloured (L91);
- tyres 185 R 14C/tyres 7.00-14 8 PR;
- inscription of the tyre pressure on the body above the wheels;
- chassis plate with 'Type 21F' stamped on it;
- higher front bumpers, and for T2b also no deformation element;
- hatch without window (M127);
- back-up lamps (T2a: M47, T2b: M616);
- radio-suppressed windscreen-wiper motor;
- additional turn signal lamps on the roof, rear (M546);
- rear mud flaps (M074);
- blue rotating light (M160);
- chrome hubcaps;
- brake booster and dual break control light (M506);
- sliding door and hatch not lockable.

Higher front bumper T2a.

Typical fire brigade equipment.

Higher front bumper T2b.

Interior

- folding seat in the load department;
- fibreboard panels on the hatch and sliding door;
- power outlet for charging the battery;
- mountings for first aid kit (M082);
- full-width metal partition between cabin and load compartment (M500);
- single seat instead of two-person passenger seat and aerial wiring, spare tyre in the cabin (M259, from model year 1972 on);
- hot-air outlet in front side of cargo compartment (M505);
- celluloid bag on the inner passenger door;
- warning triangle;
- laminated windscreen glass.

The VW Fire Truck is used mostly by town and borough councils, and companies that need to have their own fire-fighting services. Both variants, the TSF (T) and the Fire Truck with dry-powder extinguisher fittings, had no further equipment inside. The vehicles were completed afterwards by conversion firms such as Ziegler, Metz or Bachert.

The mobile pump of the TSF version was often powered by VW industrial engines. Some of the VW Fire Trucks received a luggage rack for transporting the entire technical equipment. Due to the enormous weight of the equipment and the engine-powered water pump, no more than three firefighters could be carried on board. With a change in the German DIN (German industry standard) requirements, in 1972, VW had to guarantee that the fire truck could carry no more than two people (M259).

The front of the fire brigade version has some obvious differences compared with the 'normal' Panelvan. The front bumper was raised in order to be able to drive up a steeper slope – necesary due to the German legislation in the DIN-Norm, which also prohibited a steering/ignition lock in fire trucks (M248).

With the introduction of the new DIN standard in the mid-1970s in Germany, the VW Fire Truck lost signification.

VW Crew Kombi

Many fire brigades used the VW Kombi to carry a large number of firemen from one place to another. These Bay Windows were mostly eight-seater Buses (Type 22) and seem to be similar to the standard Kombis.

The VW Crew Kombi corresponds to the DIN 14 502.

VW Commando Kombi

The VW Commando Kombi was a multi-purpose vehicle. Fire brigades of big cities or county authorities bought this variation of the T2, to use as a mobile command vehicle. It was equipped with two benches on either side of a table, with a transistor lamp above, which meant that firefighters could be instructed via radio-telephone from inside the Bus.

The VW Commando Kombi corresponded to German DIN 14 505.

T2a Crew Kombi (MS).

Charging socket 12V in the leg room.

Folding seat in the loading department.

Standard Equipment of the VW Crew Kombi

Exterior

- paint colour: body Fire Brigade Red L256 (RAL 3000); bumpers and wheels black (L41); from 1973 on, bumpers white (RAL 9010), wheels chrome-coloured (L91);
- tyres 185 R 14C/tyres 7.00-14 8 PR;
- higher front bumpers, and for T2b also no deformation element;
- inscription of the tyre pressure on the body above the wheels;
- reversing lights (installed in the tail-light) (M616, up from model year 73);
- radio suppressed windscreen-wiper motor;
- additional turn signal lamps on the roof, rear (M546);
- rear mud flaps (M074);
- blue rotating light (M160);
- chrome hubcaps.

Interior

- floor cover (rubber mat) in passenger compartment (M066);
- fibreboard panels on the hatch and sliding door;
- power outlet for charging the battery;
- mountings for first aid kit (M082);
- full-width metal partition between cabin and load compartment (M500);
- single seat instead of two-person passenger seat and aerial wiring, spare tyre in the cabin (M259, from model year 1972 on);
- hot-air outlet in front side of cargo compartment (M505);
- celluloid bag on the inner passenger door; warning triangle;
- laminated windscreen glass.

Equipment of the VW Commando Kombi

Exterior

- paint colour: body Fire Brigade Red L256 (RAL 3000); bumpers and wheels black (L41); from 1973 on, bumpers white (RAL 9010), wheels chrome-coloured (L91);
- tyres 185 R 14C/tyres 7.00-14 8 PR;
- higher front bumper, and for T2b also no deformation element;
- inscription of the tyre pressure on the body above the wheels;
- back-up lamps (T2a: M47; T2b: M616);
- radio-suppressed windscreen-wiper motor;
- additional turn signal lamps on the roof, rear (M546);
- rear mud flaps (M074);
- blue rotating light (M160);
- chrome hubcaps.

Interior

- Eberspächer petrol heater;
- fibreboard panels on the hatch and sliding door;
- power outlet for charging the battery;
- full-width metal partition between cabin and load compartment (M500);
- single seat instead of two-person passenger seat and aerial wiring, spare tyre in the cabin (M259, from model year 1973 on);
- celluloid bag on the inner passenger door;
- laminated windscreen glass;
- partially factory-prepared for radio traffic (M623);
- three-seater bench, turned around, with hinged rear seat backrest on the side of the sliding door;
- one folding table;
- one transistor lamp;
- floor cover (rubber mat) in passenger compartment (M628).

- M064 (without side gates and tailgate);
- M263 (payload of 1,200kg instead of 1,000kg).

Designated for quick-rescue purposes, the new *Schnellbergungsfahrzeug* was used in case of accidents and for technical aid. People trapped inside cars, for example, were released from dangerous situations with special emergency shears carried on board of the vehicle.

The body on the platform was made out of light aluminium and used practical roller blinds. A large, integrated luggage rack was fixed on to the roof top.

The quick-rescue vehicle contained the following basic equipment:

T2b double cab Pick-Up with construction 'Weinsberg' (JW).

T2a Fire-Chief command vehicle (MS).

T2a Pick-Up Ladder Truck (MS).

FIRE BRIGADE LADDER TRUCK

A number of fire brigades also purchased the Ladder Truck with swivelling ladders, converted by Meyer (Hagen). The basic model was a Type 261 Pick-Up.

FIRE BRIGADE PICK-UP AND DOUBLE-CAB PICK-UP TRUCKS

The T2 Pick-Up or double-cab Pick-Up Buses were infrequently used by fire brigades – the most commonly used models were always the Fire Trucks and the Crew Kombis – but some did find their way into departments in big towns or companies. They were used mostly for transport purposes.

SCHNELLBERGUNGSFAHRZEUG (QUICK-RESCUE VEHICLES)

German company Weinsberg engineered a *Schnellbergungsfahrzeug* (literally, 'quick-rescue vehicle') based on a T2 Pick-Up or double-cab Pick-Up in 1978. These two versions had the following special equipment ex works:

- M057 (hardwood strips for flatbed not fastened to vehicle);

- three floodlight lamps (1);
- hydraulic pump unit (2);
- emergency spreader (3);
- emergency shears (4);
- tools and emergency equipment (5);
- power generator (6);
- stretcher (7);
- power saw (8);
- parting-off grinder (9);
- hydraulic emergency set (10);
- two fire extinguishers (11);
- water extinguisher (12);
- 50m wire (13).

The concept for the *Schnellbergungsfahrzeug* had been developed in 1974 by the Björn Steiger Foundation and the fire department of Stuttgart to achieve a better and more effective emergency aid. The Foundation made this conversion concept very popular and bought some of the Buses for fire brigades or rescue units, financed by donations. The major advantage of the T2-based Buses was that they were agile and small. In the case of an emergency they were able to reach all areas of the production grounds within minutes, where big fire

ABOVE: T2b of the Offenbach Fire Brigade (UM).

FAR LEFT: Back with hydraulic pump unit (BS).

LEFT: Power generator and 50m wire (BS).

BELOW: T2b double-cab Pick-Up donated by Björn Steiger Foundation (BS).

T2b Pick-Up with construction 'Weinsberg' of the VW fire department.

ABOVE: *T2b double-cab Pick-Up conversion (MS).*   BELOW: *Back of the T2b double-cab Pick-Up (MS).*

trucks were not able to go, due to their size.

The 'ahead' emergency vehicles from Weinsberg were used in all Volkswagen factories in Germany.

SPECIAL CONVERSIONS

Based on a double-cab Pick-Up, the English T2b shown here was purpose-built by a special conversion firm. The double cab has two blue rotating lights and a ladder attached to the roof. Two searchlights were located on the back of the body assembly.

The fire-fighting equipment is located in the back of the fire truck, giving easy access to the water pump and hoses in case of emergency.

Shown below is a very unusual conversion – a T2a Clipper fire truck used by the company Degussa, fitted with a non-VW upper division between cabin and cargo compartment, a large roof-rack and a searchlight on the front. One notable feature is the power connection instead of the rear ventilation window.

TOP: *T2a Clipper Fire Truck Degussa (MS).*
MIDDLE: *Back of the Degussa Fire Truck (MS).*
BOTTOM: *T2 Pick-Up (Brazil) conversion (AG).*

T2a Ambulance.

T2b Ambulance.

T2a Ambulance (MS).

Front of the T2a Ambulance (MS).

AMBULANCES

One of the first special conversions of the Bus was the Krankenwagen (ambulance). From October 1950 onwards, Miesen, a company specializing in medical vehicles, built ambulances based on normal Kombis (Type 23). Almost a year later, Volkswagen took the ambulance, the designated Type 27, into its sales programme.

The VW Krankenwagen could carry up to three patients at a time. The medical services could rely on a stretcher made out of light metal, an upholstered litter and an upholstered seat with folding armrest. For reasons of hygiene, the passenger section was fitted out with a linoleum floor, which was easily cleaned.

VW thought about practical ways to store the equipment and gave the Type 27 an extra storage area with cabinet and drawers for medicine and first aid supplies. Other items of basic equipment for the ambulance included the electric rotary fresh-air fan on the roof, the sliding step under the sliding door and the sliding window between the rear department and the driver's cabin.

With the first model change in VW's history, the Ambulance was immediately available, from 1967 on. The model code did not change and they continued to be named Type 271 for LHD and Type 274 for RHD.

Typical customers in Germany for these Buses were city and county authorities, emergency services (Red Cross and German relief organizations such as Malteser-Hilfsdienst, Johanniter Unfallhilfe, Arbeiter Samariterbund and Deutsche Lebensrettungsgesellschaft), large companies that needed to have their own medical service unit, and the police.

The Type 274 ambulance shown on top left is waiting for transportation to its final destination. For transport safety reasons, the hubcaps, windscreen wipers and the blue rotation light have not yet been fitted. Typically, VW would attach the logos for large organizations while the vehicle was still in the factory. This T2 was delivered without foglamps in the front bumpers and the sliding door is on the left side.

The Type 271 for the German market had a certain standard equipment called 'Normausrüstung Krankentransportwagen nach DIN 75 080', indicated by M-code M150.

Special Models

The factory-built Type 271 (LHD) and 274 (RHD) were not the only ambulances available that were based on the Bus of the second generation. Some conversion firms specialized in producing medical vehicles too, most notably Miesen, Binz and Weinsberg.

The doctor's car shown here, of the Red Cross Esslingen, was used to care for babies in an emergency situation. Equipped by the body construction firm

Standard Ambulance equipment

Exterior

- paint colour Ivory L567 (RAL 1014), bumpers white (RAL 9010);
- illuminated sign on roof;
- searchlight;
- two reversing lights;
- hazard warning lights;
- sliding step under the sliding door;
- mud flaps;
- windscreen made out of multi-layer glass;
- outside rear-view mirrors left and right;
- electric rotary fresh-air fan in the roof;
- radial-ply tyres.

Interior

- upholstery/interior grey;
- light metal stretcher;
- upholstered litter;
- upholstered seat with folding armrest;
- upholstered seat with folding back (emergency seat);
- sliding window between rear department and driver's cabin;
- neon lamp in the rear bay;
- three-quarter frosted glass in the rear bay;
- hooks for medical bottles;
- window bars on the rear window;
- linoleum covering for floor and platform;
- cabinet and drawer for first aid supplies and utensils.

Electric rotary fresh-air fan on the roof.

Front bumper with integrated foglamps.

If they wanted to receive a grant for buying a new ambulance from the local German authorities, relief organizations or fire brigades were required to order specific equipment together with M150 (Normausrüstung). This involved the following equipment:

- two foglamps in the front bumper (1968–72), respectively on the front bumper (1973–79);
- protective undercoating;
- tyre pressure indication above the front wheels;
- holder for special equipment;
- clear battery housing.

VW made it possible for relief organizations worldwide to order the following logos fixed on to the roof as an optional extra:

- M033 – Red crescent sign instead of the Red Cross lamp (foreign countries);
- M718 – illuminated Maltese or Red Cross sign on roof;
- S768 – illuminated Maltese Cross sign on roof.

T2b Kombi baby-emergency doctor's car.

T2b Kombi baby-emergency doctor's car.

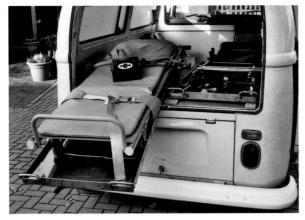

Utila stretcher (APS).

Cabinet and drawer for first aid supplies and utensils (APS).

T2a Kombi of the Dutch Police (KLN).

T2b Kombi criminal investigation department (MS).

Karosseriebau Weinsberg, it was based on a T2b Kombi model year 1978, and had an intensive nursing transportable incubator and two sliding doors, not often used for the ambulance.

POLICE VEHICLES

The T2 was the most popular 'light commercial' police car of the 1970s. In Germany it was the standard vehicle in nearly every federal state and the VW Kombi remains the 'standard' Police Bus today. The advantages of the VW Transporter were its low purchase costs, its robustness and the wide range of variations. The Police Kombi was used in many different situations, for example, as a road traffic accident emergency vehicle, prisoner transporter, patrol car, radar-control vehicle, crew transporter or scene-of-crime vehicle of the criminal investigation department. These Buses were mostly equipped with a blue rotating light (M160), sirens and special suppression equipment, prepared for radio traffic (M623).

Few Police Buses were ordered as Panelvans. This model type was used only for transportation purposes or as an observation vehicle. The federal states in Germany had to have their own riot police and every squadron had to have at least its own medical service vehicle. For this they mostly used the factory-built Ambulance Type 27, with Ivory body paint. The typical red cross signage was replaced by a white cross in a green square.

The T2b 'criminal investigation department Kombi' shown, was used for observation purposes. It was a standard Kombi with a blue rotating light, additional windscreen washers (M288), two halogen foglamps on the front (M659), and a Westfalia roof-rack with telescopic ladder.

Vehicle conversions such as prisoner transporters, radar speed traps, loudspeaker Buses or those used by the criminal investigation departments, were carried out by special manufacturers.

Road Traffic Accident Emergency Vehicle

The road traffic accident emergency vehicle shown was offered by VW directly. It was orderable as a SO3 Kombi with a mobile office, converted by Westfalia.

T2b Police Kombi with typical equipment.

Interior

- Eberspächer petrol heater (M119);
- fibreboard panels on the hatch and sliding door;
- full-width metal partition between cabin and load compartment (M500);
- single seat instead of two-person passenger seat and aerial wiring, spare tyre in the cabin (M259, from model year 1973 on);
- laminated windscreen glass;
- partially factory-prepared for radio traffic (M623) (customer outlet, Ambulance/Fire Brigade section);
- three-seater bench, turned around, with hinged rear seat backrest on the side of the sliding door;
- one folding table;
- one transistor lamp;
- floor cover (rubber mat) in passenger compartment (M628);
- optional: upper partition between cabin and passenger compartment with sliding window (M523; only with M500).

Exterior

- roof-rack with telescopic ladder;
- blue rotating light with sirens (M160).

ABOVE: T2a/b Kombi road traffic accident emergency vehicle of the Neumünster police (PSH).
LEFT: T2b Kombi Loudspeaker Vehicle of the Karlsruhe police (UM).

Accessories such as road signs, lamps, police signalling disc, reflective clothing, accident set with camera, flashing signal lamps, distance-measuring instrument and first aid kit did not belong to the basic SO3 equipment of Westfalia. They were bought and fitted in by the police themselves.

The police of the Federal State of Schleswig-Holstein ordered some specially equipped Kombis in the early 1970s. Based on the regular SO3 with a mobile office, the Buses were fitted out with the following additional features:

- a special roof-rack with three orange warning lights, which could be used to warn other drivers;
- a foglamp on the engine lid;
- extendable blue rotation light fixed on the front of the roof-rack instead of the normal one, which was positioned in the middle of the roof over the driver's cabin;

- painted red and white stripes on both edges at the back of the Bus.

Mobile Radar Speed Trap

One interesting conversion was the T2b Kombi Radar Bus of the Bavarian Police in Munich. It differed from earlier mobile speed-trap conversions, which had

T2b Radar speed trap with opened 'front-door' and radar unit (PM).

three-quarters of the front side cut off, including the window; this T2b Radar Bus was modified only from the front grille to the bumper to install a hinged front-opening door on the right side. The advantage of this construction was that the windscreen did not have to be modified, making the whole conversion much cheaper than the earlier ones.

Mounted on small rails, the radar unit could be used in two ways:

- as a roadside system, with the Bus being parked in position and the radar unit used through the open 'front door';
- as a free-standing system outside the Bus, for example, over a motorway bridge.

The Bay Window Kombi mobile-office vehicle, Type 2310, was often used as a mobile radar speed trap. This type was equipped with a folding table, turned-around benches in the passenger compartment, floor cover and a transistor lamp over the middle window above the left side of the table.

T2b Kombi of the Neumünster Police (PSH).

At the Highway Police Station in Bad Oldeslohe (PSH).

ABOVE: T2b Kombi with bike on trailer of the Neumünster police (PSH).

RIGHT: T2b Kombi of the riot Police (left), and T2b patrol Bus (PSH).

BELOW: T2b Kombi without rotation light at a demonstration in Brockdorf (PSH).

T2a Kombi of the Bavarian riot police at the Munich Olympic Stadium (PM).

T2b Loudspeaker vehicle of the Hamburg Police.

Kombi Loudspeaker Vehicle

Ordered by the German Ministry of Internal Affairs (destination code 908), the T2b Kombi shown here was built on 25 October 1978 on chassis number 2182 041 440. The Bus left the Hannover factory to go to F.X. Kögel, a company specializing in building loudspeaker vehicles, where it was fitted with some additional equipment that was not available from VW. None of these parts is identifiable from the M-Plate.

The Bus had four small holders beside each window. Extra plastic windows or grilles could be attached to these holders, as protection against demonstrators.

This green T2b Kombi was handed over to Hamburg Police department several months after it had been fully equipped. It was then registered in Hamburg with the licence plate HH-3772, as part of the riot-police squadron.

The Loudspeaker Bus appeared on television in the German thriller *Tatort*, in the episode 'Ein Wodka zu viel'. In 2001, it was bought by the German club 'Community of Interest T2'. It has since been restored and received its old Hamburg police stickers on each front door.

In model year 1978, group codes CN9, H21 and KC3 represented the following groups of M-codes:

- CN9 = M066, M082, M089, M102, M186;
- H21 = M103, M161, M172, M184, M227, M506, M507, M508;
- KC3 = M032, M060, M121, M206, M503.

This Kombi has a 2000cc engine with 70bhp.

M-Plate of the Loudspeaker Vehicle

```
82  044  410
531 551 597 616 623
984677  CN9  H21 KC3 Z01
43 3  7371  908  2316  31
```

Plate of the converter F.X. Kögel.

Additional equipment on Kombi Loudspeaker Vehicle

Exterior

- two sirens on the front bumper;
- two removable blue rotating lights;
- extra spray nozzles;
- flag holder on the driver's side;
- five rotatable loudspeakers on the roof.

Interior

- lateral flap on the driver's side for external power supply, separate electric meter;
- table in the passenger compartment with tuner, cassette deck and two microphones;
- small map light beneath the glove box

TOP LEFT: Flag holder.
TOP RIGHT: Extra spray nozzles.
BOTTOM LEFT: Foglamps and sirens.
BOTTOM RIGHT: Loudspeakers.

T2 ARMOURED MONEY TRANSPORTERS

A non-standard SO model was converted by Karosserie- und Fahrzeugwerke Wilhelm Thiele as a vehicle for the transportation of money or valuables. The Bremen specialist was the official partner of the Volkswagenwerk AG for such conversions, turning serial T2 Panelvans into Money Transporters. These were identified by M-code S712 ('factory-prepared for conversion to armoured money transporter').

One typical feature of the early Thiele conversions of the T2 (model year 1969) was the windscreen, which was made up of two separated sections of 27mm bullet-proof glass, instead of the serial 'panorama'-style screen. From model year 1970 on, the Armoured Money Transporter had a bullet-proof windscreen styled like the serial one. This kind of glass was resistant against shots from a 9mm pistol, such as a 3.57 Magnum.

All the doors and underneath the front were armoured on the inside with 3mm steel sheet (St 52). The doors had supplementary push bolts on their inner sides. An extra safety lock was installed below the left side of the sliding door, but the T2 Money Transporter had no protection below on the chassis side.

Depending on clients' needs, the Money Transporter was available with an extra bench in the cargo department, allowing it to carry three or four security guards, including the driver. Buses used for long-distance trips had an additional safe right on the platform inside over the engine.

Optional Extras

From model year 1971 on, the T2 Money Transporter could be ordered with a special airconditioning unit, positioned on the back of the roof. This extra feature was a must, especially in the summer, because none of the windows could be opened and the air valve in the front was welded shut to prevent anyone discharging a poisonous substance into the Bus.

To get the money quickly and safely inside the Transporter, there was a very

1969: T2a Thiele Money Transporter (WT).

Armoured door with bullet-proof glass (WT).

1970: T2a Thiele Money Transporter (WT).

Bench in the cargo compartment (WT).

Airconditioned Money Transporter (WT).

Armoured door in the sliding door (WT).

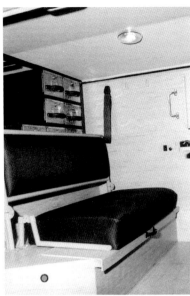

Bench in the cargo compartment (WT).

Safe (WT).

Prevention: mirrors at the back (WT).

helpful optional extra in the form of a small armoured door in the sliding door. This could be bolted only from the inside.

A number of the Bay Window Money Transporters had a device for money trunks right at the back over the engine. They could be set in only by opening the rear panel. A big rear-view mirror was placed on each side, right beneath the engine air-intake louvres, for the driver to see if anyone was standing behind the Bus.

All the T2 Armoured Money Transporters had a bench seat for the security

guards in the cargo compartment. For transporting special goods such as jewellery, gold and so on, this seat was foldable and lockable. It therefore was able to function as a safe, which was welded to the body of the vehicle.

NWSG

The first Money Transporter based on a T2a was delivered to the Niedersächsische Wach- und Schliessgesellschaft company in Hannover, the very first private firm involved in transporting money in Germany. Their Money Transporters were finished in dark blue on the body, while the roof was white. This colour combination was very unusual for a Panelvan.

Latin American version

Two special variants of the Money Transporter were built in 1969, based on a T2a, and in 1973, based on T2b. These were conversions for Latin

America, ordered by the exclusive importer for that region, VW Interamericana. (For all the export destinations from this importer, *see* Chapter 9.) The Latin Americans ordered fifteen to twenty Buses in this special conversion. The business was handled by the German office of VW Interamericana, located in the 'Chile-House' in Hamburg.

Constructed to suit the particular requirements of this region, the Money Transporters sold by VW Interamericana had additional safety equipment, including a sort of metal shield protecting the wheels from bullets.

Instead of a sliding door, the T2a Money Transporter had a small 'normal' door giving access to the cargo compartment, with an additional door for the intake of the money. Positioned on the roof, an electric ventilator moved in fresh air. There was a single siren on the roof, too. In addition, this Transporter had the special feature of a small window made out of bullet-proof glass on each side with a crenel underneath.

LEFT: T2a NWSG Money Transporter in Hannover (NW).
ABOVE: Latin American conversion, from inside (WT).

T2b version with wheel protection (WT).

T2a Latin American version (WT).

T2b version without wheel protection (WT).

T2b Bischoff & Hamel conversion (BH).

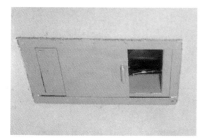

Ventilation system in the driver's cabin (BH).

Storage space with spare wheel (BH).

Dashboard: button to activate the electromagnetic door lock (BH).

Safety door (BH).

could be activated by a combined system of manual and electromagnetic features. In addition, the driver's cabin was equipped with an installation traffic and an alarm system. Big exterior rear-view mirrors on both cabin doors ensured a good view of the back.

The interior, especially the cargo compartment, was sheathed with special steel sheets and electrostatic flocked. The windscreen and the cabin-door windows were made out of four-pane bullet-proof glass additionally mounted from the outside. The Armoured Money Transporter had no sliding doors but could be loaded via a sideways revolving door, which could only be opened from the inside. The door hinges were inside.

Also available as extra options were airconditioning, Eberspächer auxiliary heating and an optical alarm system.

MILITARY MODELS

Nearly every armed force in Western Europe used the second-generation VW Transporter in its numerous military variations. As a mobile radio-control vehicle, ambulance, fire truck or personnel carrier, the T2 was the most-used light commercial vehicle.

As with the T1 military models, factory-fitted M-codes were normally specified on the Bay Window Buses, too. The most frequently used M-codes were Eberspächer heater, front and rear towing hook and radio interference suppression; these were painted rather than chrome parts.

German Army

The German Army ordered huge numbers of Kombis and double-cab Pick-Up Buses. The other types, such as the

Bischoff & Hamel Conversion

Another company specializing in converting serial Bay Window Buses into armoured money transporters was the Hannover manufacturer Bischoff & Hamel, well known as a Volkswagen dealer (destination code 024) to this day.

The armoured money transporters of Bischoff & Hamel differed from the serial T2 in that they were fitted out with equipment for radio traffic, a ventilation system in the driver's cabin, an extra storage space with a place for the spare wheel, and two buttons on the dashboard to activate the electromagnetic door lock.

The standard mounted doors in the cabin were armour-plated and had an additional safety locking device. This lock

Standard equipment for German Army Buses

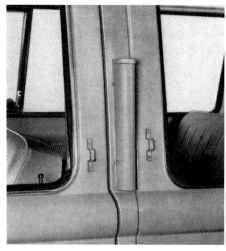

Flag holder.

Exterior

- flag holder on the left side;
- front and rear towing hook (M029) (T2a and T2a/b);
- special colour RAL 6014;
- two windows in the rear side gates;
- blanket covers for camouflage: casing for external rear mirrors, windscreen, side and rear windows and headlamps;
- tilt and bows in colour RAL 6014 (double-cab Pick-Up).

Interior

- radio suppressed according to German Army prescriptions (M623);
- transparent battery case;
- Eberspächer heater BN4 (M119);
- one single seat and a two-seater bench in the passenger compartment (Type 265);
- two gun racks, on the left and right side of the dashboard and the cabin ground;
- holder for first-aid kit;
- holder for fire extinguisher;
- holder for decontamination kit;
- holder for warning triangle under the dashboard (T2a and T2a/b), later, in a case under the passenger seat (T2b);

Gun rack.

Holder for decontamination kit, holder for warning triangle and stop block.

C-rails in the passenger compartment.

German Army specification: tailgate with windows for tail-lights.

T2b Kombi German Army.

- Stop block fixed in the engine bay (T2a and T2a/b), from later on behind the passenger seat (T2b);
- C-rails (Type 23): in the passenger compartment, four fitted on the cargo floor, two on the left inner body panel (maximum load 2 × 25kg) and two parallel for each division wall behind driver's and passengers' seat (maximum load 25kg for each side);
- C-rails over the engine compartment: four fitted on the floor;
- C-rails (Type 265) on the platform: four fitted on the platform, two rails at the inside of each side gate (maximum load 2 x 25kg);
- C-rails in the passenger compartment: two on the partition between driver and passenger compartment and two behind the single seat on the back panel.

T2b prototype Pick-Up of the German Army.

single-cab Pick-Up trucks and Panelvans, did not play a part in the fleet of the German Army.

Swiss Army

As well as having the well-known variations of Kombi models, the Swiss Army also had a couple of high-roof Panelvans in service that it used as a dark room for developing pictures in the field. The vehicles had baths for development liquid inside and were 100 per cent isolated against sunlight. The T2 shown here, owned by Tom van Wissen, is one of four Swiss Army Buses that are known still to exist from model year 1969; all have the same features, including the typical army equipment of an Eberspächer BN4 heater. The chrome parts, the high roof and the rims were all painted in Army Green. On regular series production, the high roof could only be ordered in white.

One special feature of this Bus is the camouflage light on the left side of the front right, next to the headlight (shown uncovered here). Another interesting detail is the lockable power connection on the left outer body side, right beneath the rear tyre.

POSTAL SERVICES

Since the early 1950s, Volkswagen products have been used by postal fleets all across Europe. As early as the 1960s, VW had responded to the requirements of the postal services and had developed a high-roof Panelvan, thereby creating more space to enable a driver to transport more goods on each trip.

T2a Kombi German Army with blanket covers for camouflage.

T2b Double-Cab Pick-Up German Army with blanket covers for camouflage.

German Postal Services

Particularly in Germany, the VW Transporter of the second generation had a key position in postal services. The Deutsche Bundespost (German federal post) used it in various guises and for various purposes. The high-roof Panelvan was ideal for the delivery of packages, while the Kombi served for group transportation. In the fleet of the Deutsche Bundespost the VW T2 was the perfect addition to the Beetle and the VW 147 'Fridolin', used for delivering the 'classic' mail, and the big trucks that were used for transporting parcels over long distances.

One way to distinguish between the different postal sectors was by the

exterior body colour. In general, all vehicles for the delivery of parcels/letters and for radio measurement were painted yellow. The telecommunications transporters were distinguished by their dark grey body colour.

All postal service Buses were finished with adhesive decals, fixed in the VW factory. The T2s of the 'yellow' post got the lettering 'Deutsche Bundespost' and a pictogram with a post horn (M109). The telecommunications vehicles were marked with 'Deutsche Bundespost', the post horn and the extra lettering 'Fernmeldedienst' ('telecommunications department') (M131). Panelvans with or without a high roof often had lettering indicating maximum axle loads and maximum weight (M065).

Swiss Army.

Swiss Army.

M-Plate of the Swiss Army High-Roof Panelvan

```
25 6
501  514  726  794
11  376  100  119  127
SZ  2113  5217269216057
```

Swiss Army.

T2a Panelvan – German Mail.

T2a Panelvan – German Mail telecommunication department.

T2b Panelvan.

T2a Panelvan with high roof.

PANELVANS

Soon after the first model change in the history of Volkswagen, a huge number of Panelvans were introduced into the post fleet for delivery services and telecommunications. The Panelvans shown here date from model year 1971. They can be easily dated by their flat hubcaps, which became standard in this year with the introduction of the disc brake.

The Panelvan shown on top left had a device for a lock fixed between the B-pillar and the sliding door. Such Bay Windows were used for the transportation of insured parcels and letters.

Panelvans of the German federal post that were used for deliveries were often fitted with a partition between the cabin and the cargo compartment,

to prevent the load sliding through. The Bus shown above left had an upper partition between cabin and cargo compartment (M510); this sort of equipment is very rare.

In January 1968 the high-roof Panelvan completed the Volkswagen sales programme. All Transporters of this type had a high bulkhead with a middle passage, a high sliding door and two single seats in the cabin. In contrast to the predecessor of the T2, the material for the high roof was fibreglass, less weighty than the steel that had been used on the high roof of the T1. Consequently, the T2 Panelvan with high roof allowed for a higher payload than the T1 in the same design.

The T2a high-roof Panelvan shown here has a partition made of wood in

the cargo compartment. This feature, fitted in the Hannover factory, prevented parcels from falling while keeping the sliding door open for loading and unloading (M544).

From 1973 on, the revised model, the T2b, was introduced for all German post services. In operation until approximately 1985, these Transporters were recognizable by the new turn signals right under the windscreen and the new front bumper with deformation element.

KOMBI

In comparison with the other model types, the T2 Kombi was only ordered in small numbers by the Deutsche Bundespost. They were mainly used by the telecommunications department for group transportation, to bring employees to, or from, their workplace.

On the telecommunications side, the T2 was often used as a *Peilwagen* (literally 'locating vehicle'), equipped with a special antenna on its rooftop. The disassembly or conversion was carried out by specialist firms.

The T2a Kombi shown here was built in model year 1968 (identifiable by a door handle with press button). It was probably a sample vehicle for the Deutsche Bundespost.

T2b Panelvan with high roof.

T2a Kombi with single passenger seats in the cabin and spare tyre in the back.

T2a Kombi Funkmessdienst.

T2b Kombi as measuring vehicle with two antennas (MS).

Interior with single seat (MS).

Front with original 'Deutsche Bundespost' number plate (MS).

PICK-UP AND DOUBLE-CAB PICK-UP

One very rare vehicle in the fleet of the Deutsche Bundespost was the Pick-Up Transporter, which operated in the area of telecommunications. The fleet's Pick-Up and double-cab Pick-Up Transporters were usually used for the transportation of telecommunication cables.

Swiss Postal Services (PTT)

The design of the vehicles in service with the Swiss PTT is well known; shown here is a T2a Panelvan used for parcel and letter delivery. Up to the roll underneath the windows, these Bay Window Buses were painted yellow; the roll itself was red and the section above it was white. The PTT logo was fixed on both front doors. All these Buses had chrome hubcaps.

BELOW LEFT: T2b Pick-Up 'Fernmeldedienst' (JW).
BELOW: Model year 1971: T2a Panelvan as parcel delivery van with roof rack of the Swiss post (JW).

T2b Panelvan disaster prevention, North Rhine-Westphalia.

T2b Kombi disaster prevention, North Rhine-Westphalia.

Flag holder for trips in a convoy.

Signalling disk.

RELIEF ORGANIZATIONS

Relief organizations all over the world relied for many years on the VW Transporter and its various types, and many T2 Buses remained on duty until at least the 1990s.

Deutsches Rotes Kreuz (German Red Cross)

The Red Cross is the largest relief organization in the world. The German branch, the DRK (Deutsches Rotes Kreuz), owned an enormous fleet of T2 Transporters in the 1970s, with every type of Bay Window Bus being used at some time for some purpose. The fleet included T2 Ambulances for the carrying of injured persons, double-cab Pick-Up Buses for transportation purposes, Panelvans for blood donor transportation, or disaster prevention, Kombis for moving disabled people, schoolchildren or senior citizens. It seems that there was a VW Transporter that was right for every situation.

All the DRK Buses had an illuminated roof sign with a Red Cross on it (S718). The body colour of almost all Buses was Ivory L567 (RAL 1014), although some Bay Windows of the blood donor unit were painted grey or blue.

1979 Panelvan DRK NRW

M-Plate of the T2b Panelvan DRK NRW

```
92 005 678
502  510 616 640 718
9115NP  F60 H82 065 237
03 2  7134  133  2110  11
```

F60 = M100, M172
H82 = M161, M184, M500, M503

1979 Kombi DRK NRW

M-Plate of the T2b Kombi DRK NRW

```
92 157 671
640  718 731 746 777
9115NP  GKL HAD HX3 060
18 4  7348  133  2316  11
```

GKL = M503, M551, M616
HAD = M066, M100, M500, M623
HX3 = M161, M172, M184, M186, M225, M227

Side view (above right) and front view (right) of T2b Kombi DRK Hildesheim.

1974 Kombi DRK Hildesheim – A Red Cross Bus story

Soon after the re-establishment of the DRK in 1973 in Söhlde (near Salzgitter), the former chairwoman, Sister Erika, and the other active helpers received their new Kombi. The asset costs were divided between the DRK and the township of Söhlde. Right from the first day, the Bus was cherished. The DRK group travelled several times to Friedland, carrying clothes and groceries to one of the biggest reception camps in Germany, as well as going to Hannover airport, Hamburg, the North Sea coast, and so on. The longest trip the Bus made was to a summer camp in Finland in 1980, but its main purpose was always to carry older people of the community to the senior citizens' evening every week.

The T2b Kombi served the DRK for twenty-five years, covering 45,000km, until it was bought by a member of the German Community of Interest T2 (IG T2) in the summer of 1998. One year later, it became a part of the IG T2 collection.

M-Plate of the Kombi DRK Hildesheim

```
42 012 158
208  500 504 549 718
911551  E13 119 141 160
35 3  7490  025  2312  11
```

E13 = M055, M066, M507, M511, M616

Open lid with UTILA-stretcher.   *Fire extinguisher inside.*

DEUTSCHES ROTES KREUZ
KREISVERBAND
HILDESHEIM-MARIENBURG

DRK lettering on the front doors.

T2a Double-Cab Pick-Up UN (JW).

THW half-Panelvan (S756) (UM).

United Nations (UN)

In 1974 a T2a double-cab Pick-Up was used by the United Nations to provide UN troops in the demilitarized zone in the Sinai desert with a supply of drinking water. The Bus had a rotating blue light with sirens (M160) and foglamps above the front bumper. Interestingly, it had a wiper missing on the passenger side. UN vehicles were painted white and had the UN logo on the front doors. This special Bus had 'Trinkwasser' ('drinking water') lettering on its side doors.

Technisches Hilfswerk (THW)

In August 1950 the German Ministry of Internal Affairs established the 'Technisches Hilfswerk' ('technical aid service'), consisting of German volunteers, to give technical help in disaster prevention and in extreme emergency situations. The most frequently used light commercial vehicle at the THW from the 1950s to the 1980s was the VW Kombi, assigned as a kind of multi-purpose vehicle for the transportation of devices and crews. Nearly all such Bay Window Buses were painted dark blue.

Some units of the THW had special Buses that were produced exclusively for the German Ministry of Internal Affairs. The radio units used so-called 'half Panelvans', painted orange and with white lettering on them. These Bay Windows were equipped with a window in the sliding door and in its opposite side (S756). The rear panel lid had no window (M127). A typical feature on these radio Buses was the two aerials in the back, mounted on the rear bumper and the air-intake louvres. On the driver's side over the rear wheel, a lateral flap for an external power supply was installed. Inside, the Bus was equipped with two benches facing each other

ABOVE: T2b Double-Cab Pick-Up 'THW Gifhorn' (HF).
LEFT: T2b Kombi 'THW Garmisch-Partenkirchen' (HF).

T2b Kombi 'THW Rosenheim' (HF).

1975: T2b Kombi 'THW' at a Police control (HF).

T2b Kombi with special equipment 'THW' (HF).

and a table with a transistor lamp above. Special wooden shelves were installed in the compartment in the back over the engine. All THW Buses had one or two – mostly removable – rotating lights with sirens.

The THW units also had a few T2 double-cab Pick-Ups, mostly used for transportation purposes.

Several pictures on this page, taken by THW member Hansjörg Frick, show the T2 Kombis of the THW Rosenheim (Bavaria) at work. The Type 22 with the licence plate RO-8100 is equipped with an emergency spreader and a power generator for mechanical help at the scene of accidents. Not standard for THW Buses, this Bay Window has a searchlight and an extra siren on its roof top.

At the end of the 1970s, the German Ministry of Internal Affairs (destination code 908) ordered several hundred specially equipped Radio Buses, which were issued to every city or administrative district in Germany to be used in disaster prevention. The Bus shown here, still in use in 2004, was built on chassis number 237 2 148 818. Manufactured on 17 May 1977, it was registered over three years later on 29 September 1980. This Kombi was equipped with a modified Type 4 2000cc engine with 70bhp.

In model year 1977, the group codes RXB, SAP and SR3 represented the following M-codes:

- RXB = M032, 085, 089, 094, 121, 284, 191;
- SAP = M203, 227, 259, 500, 503, 506, 507;

T2b Kombi 'THW' Radio-Bus (ET).

Rear view with power outlet and aerial (ET).

Equipment in the rear (ET).

M-Plate of the THW Radio Bus

72 148 818
547 551 616 623 719
922490 RXB SAP SR3 060
20 2 7470 908 2310 31

Inside the cargo compartment (ET).

- SR3 = M082, 100, 102, 103, 106, 161, 172.

In spite of the huge number of M-codes, not all of the fitted equipment was described. A hint of the non-serial installations gave the S-code 719 (production number for special build-ins with documents). This code covers the mountings of the flag holder on the driver's side, blue rotating lights and sirens, the external power outlet and the whole interior in the passenger compartment. The

paint code 9224 stands for the orange paint job, but also included bumpers, VW logo, wheels and hubcaps which were all painted black.

Malteser Hilfsdienst

Founded in 1956, the Malteser Hilfsdienst is a big emergency aid organization in Germany, divided into a single diocese all over the country, each with its own vehicle fleets. The majority of the second-generation Buses in service with the organization were Kombis and Ambulances, alongside a small number of double-cab Pick-Up Buses that were used for transportation purposes. All the vehicles had an illuminated roof sign with the 'Malteser Kreuz' logo (S768) and the lettering 'Malteser Hilfsdienst' on both sides, as well as a 'Malteser Kreuz' logo on the front. The paint colour was Ivory L567 (RAL 1014) with white bumpers (RAL 9010).

1972: Presentation of the Würzburg Malteser Hilfsdienst in front of the Würzburg Residence.

1969: First ambulance for the Malteser Hilfsdienst Aschaffenburg (Bayern) (MH).

T2a/b Kombi school bus (MI I).

New ambulance for the Malteser Hilfsdienst Ebermannstadt (Bavaria) (MH).

Arbeiter Samariter Bund

T2b Ambulance: first Car for the Malteser Hilfsdienst Görlitz (Eastern Germany) after the German reunion (MH).

In 1888 six carpenters from Berlin founded the German emergency aid service Arbeiter Samariter Bund (ASB). The ASB's fields of activity ranged from ambulance and medical services to rescue and emergency. The entire fleet in the 1970s consisted of T2 Ambulances and Kombis, recognizable by the illuminated roof sign with an 'S cross' logo. All Buses were painted in Ivory L567 (RAL 1014) with white bumpers (RAL 9010), except those based in the German state of Hessen, which were varnished in green.

T2b Ambulance: evacuation of an old peoples home in Bensberg (1980) (MH).

T2a Ambulance: ASB Frankfurt (Hessen) (ASB).

T2b Ambulance: ASB Frankfurt (Hessen) (ASB).

ABOVE: *T2b Ambulance : ASB Köln (ASB).*
RIGHT: *T2a Ambulance: ASB Köln (ASB).*

New Buses for the ASB Ludwigsburg (ASB).

T2a Ambulance in action (ASB).

Front of a T2a Ambulance (ASB).

SPECIAL SALES CAMPAIGNS

In the late 1970s, the final years of the Bay Window, Volkswagen aimed to boost sales by special sales campaigns. The concept had already been used a couple of times on the Beetle (special editions included the 'Gelb Schwarze Renner' and the 'Jeans') in previous years. Special sales campaign vehicles distinguish themselves by a few factors. First, they were available for a limited period of time, usually a few months. They had a special paint colour and interior that was not available in the normal sales programme. To make these vehicles more attractive they came with a range of luxury extras as standard, all at an attractive price, of course.

Champagne Edition I (S723)

The first special sales campaign was begun in 1977 in the USA to commemorate the production of the one-millionth VW Rabbit (American VW Golf). A range of specially equipped Volkswagens appeared on the market, including a Microbus. The range was marketed under the name of 'Champagne Edition'. The special models were produced only in 1977 and sold exclusively in the USA.

The Champagne Edition I package comprised the following features:

■ a paint job in Agate Brown L86Z with Atlas White L91Z roof, Atlas White wheels, Parchment coloured interior;

■ a padded steering wheel (this became standard equipment in 1978);
■ chrome bumpers and rubber bumper strips (M162);
■ chrome trim around windows and chrome VW logo;
■ ventilation windows in passenger compartment (M508); and
■ a small round sticker below the windscreen with the VW logo surrounded by leaves, plus the words 'Champagne Edition'.

Even though this Bus was already quite comfortable, a few extras could still be ordered, including a sliding roof (M560), automatic transmission (M249) and tinted glass (M568).

The really special part of the first Champagne Edition was the interior, which was finished in Parchment, a kind of beige/yellow. The seats had corduroy upholstery in a style that had never been seen before on a Bay Window Bus. The other special feature was the unusual number of colour-coordinated interior parts: the spare-tyre cover, floor carpets, kick panels and trunk panels were all Parchment. The only example of a similarly colour-coordinated configuration was the 'Light Sand/Khaki Brown' interior fitted in the early Microbuses.

The technical specifications were the same as for most of the USA-delivered Microbuses in 1977. There was a total of seven seating places. The front seats were fitted with headrests and all seven seating places had a seatbelt. It was powered by a 2000cc 70bhp fuel-injected engine, and Buses delivered to California were equipped with a catalyst (M27) to comply with the strict exhaust-emission regulations.

The Champagne Edition Microbus was built in the period from February to April 1977.

Champagne Edition II (S765)

In spring 1978, the following headline appeared in an American VW brochure: 'VW uncorks the Champagne Edition II!' Apparently the first series of Champagnes had been successful enough for Volkswagen to consider a sequel. Like the first edition, the Champagne Edition II was available only in the USA. The range comprised the Beetle Convertible, the Rabbit (the American Golf), the Dasher (the American Passat), the Scirocco, the Bus and even a Westfalia Campmobile. The Champagne models were not very similar to each other in terms of design, except that they had a look that was exclusive within their own range. Even the two Champagne Bay Windows had little in common.

Champagne Edition II – Microbus (S765).

Champagne Edition II – Microbus (S765).

MICROBUS

The Champagne Edition II Microbus was painted Date Nut Brown LH8A with a Fox Red LH3A roof and Fox Red wheels. The exterior was finished with three stripes that went from tail-light to tail-light via the front of the Bus. The inside was finished in Sienna Red/Brown, made out of corduroy and vinyl, with seven seating places. As on the Champagne Edition I, the interior was completely colour coordinated – the carpeting, spare tyre cover, trunk panels and kick panels were all Sienna Red – but there was an extra touch in that a number of interior parts that were normally dark grey or black were now Saddle Brown. The Saddle Brown parts were the entire dashboard, the steering wheel, the ignition lock cover, the turn signal and windscreen-wiper handles, the inner rear-view mirror, the flip side of the sun visors, the wheel-arch covers, the hot-air outlet to the middle seat, the gearshift knob and the handbrake handle. On the cabin doors, the window winder, the pull strap, the release lever, the fresh-air vents, the arm rest and the fresh-air duct were all in Saddle Brown. The Saddle Brown window winder and the release lever unit were taken from the VW Rabbit and therefore had a slightly different design (*see* picture below). These parts could be easily fitted into a Bay Window, so Volkswagen probably decided not make a special brown version of them.

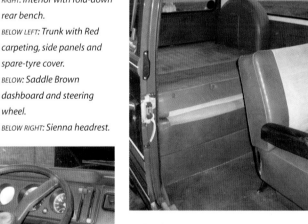

LEFT: *Two-person middle bench.*
RIGHT: *Interior with fold-down rear bench.*
BELOW LEFT: *Trunk with Red carpeting, side panels and spare-tyre cover.*
BELOW: *Saddle Brown dashboard and steering wheel.*
BELOW RIGHT: *Sienna headrest.*

Saddle Brown window winder.

Saddle Brown release lever and door strap.

The red/brown upholstery cloth has tended to fade over the years to a yellow colour (*see* the details of the Champagne Edition II interior on p.115).

The interior was so eye-catching that a casual observer might overlook all the standard extras that came with this Bus. These included tinted windows, a sliding window in the middle on both left and right, chrome trim around the windows, a chrome VW logo, a clock in the dashboard plus windscreen wipers with interval and wash-wipe function. Optional extras available for this Bus were a sliding roof (M560), an Eberspächer petrol heater (M60) and automatic transmission (M249).

The technical specifications were similar to other US-delivered Buses in 1978. It has a 2000cc 70bhp fuel-injected engine, front seats with headrests, seat belts for all seven seating places and for Californian Buses a catalyst (M27) to meet exhaust-emission regulations.

The Champagne Edition II was built during the period January to April 1978.

Westfalia Campmobile

The two-tone colour pattern of the Champagne Edition II Campmobile certainly resembled that of the Champagne Microbus from the year before. While the first Champagne Microbus had Atlas White wheels and roof, the Camper version of 1978 had them in Pastel White L90D.

The Campmobile equipment was made by Westfalia. It was finished with a brown-beige plaid that was also available outside this special sales campaign. All the parts that were Saddle Brown in the Microbus version were also used in the Campmobile, except the fresh-air duct on the cabin doors, which was not fitted. The Deluxe Camper interior type is P27, which resembles the European 'Westfalia Berlin'. The main differences are the electrical system and the spare tyre, which is in fact a folding spare tyre installed in the back on the left side. The US version was fitted with a 110V electrical system instead of the 220V system used in Europe.

The Champagne Edition II had the following standard equipment: a clock in the dashboard, swivelling passenger seat (M690), chrome bumpers, rubber bumper strips (M162), tinted glass except in the louvred side windows (M568) and interval windscreen wipers

with wash-wipe automatic (M652). The optional extra available for this Bus was automatic transmission (M249).

The technical specifications of the Champagne Edition II Westfalia were the same as those of the Microbus version.

Silberfisch (S766)

The only Bay Window sales campaign in Europe began in June 1978, two months after the last Champagne Edition II was made, and ended in November of the same year. This Bus soon became known as the Silberfisch ('Silver Fish') because of its unique silver metallic paint. Volkswagen had not produced the T2 in a metallic colour before. The Silberfisch was characterized by two black stripes under the belt line, which circled around the entire Bus, and a Marine (dark blue) eight-seater cloth interior with matching blue carpet. It was exclusively sold in West Germany.

Curiously, the Silberfisch was equipped with the ventilation windows in the back; these were officially replaced by sliding windows in August 1977.

The Silberfisch came with a wide range of extras: trip counter and clock (M25), lockable cap for fuel tank (M32), lockable glove compartment lid (M54), Braunschweig radio (M96), rear-window defogger (M102), rubber bumper strips (M162), inner rear-view mirror, anti-dazzle (M206), ventilation windows in passenger compartment (M508), padded dashboard (M511), halogen headlamps (M551), steel sliding roof (M560), back-up lamps (M616), chrome trim around windows and chrome VW logo.

Almost all Silberfisch Buses were identical and rarely came with extra options. Only one seven-seater 'Silberfisch' Bus is known (a special conversion for a handicapped person). The Silberfisch came with a 2000cc 70bhp engine with two carburettors and manual transmission.

Silberfisch (S766).

Test model of North American sales campaign. This Chrome striping was never used on any bus for the USA and Canadian market.

Jacobs fleet in front of the Bremen municipal hall (K).

transporters at work

'The VW Transporter for 1,000 and one purposes' was Volkswagen's familiar advertising slogan in the late 1950s and early 1960s, and the expansion in the range continued with the introduction of the T2 in 1967. The wide variety of models and types, established in the first generation, was continually enlarged, and Volkswagen developed some important relationships with partner companies such as Westfalia, Wiedenbrück (for mobile shops, taxis, and so on) and Dunker (for refrigeration vehicles). There was a significant boom in the key-account business, which had been an important outlet of the Volkswagenwerk right from the beginning. Entire company fleets were equipped with Bay Window Buses modulated to their specific needs. With its large carrying capacity, its efficiency and speed, the VW Transporter continued to provide the solution to ever-increasing demands for the delivery of fresh goods. Another advantage of the vehicle was the fact that the sides provided a large area for advertising.

T2a Panelvan 'Artus Quelle'.

T2b Panelvan 'Kastens Hotel'.

T2a Microbus L 'Pressetaxi'.

T2b Panelvan 'Berta Müller' (HH).

T2b Panelvan 'Berta Müller' (HH).

T2b Panelvan 'L. Pawlowsky'.

T2a Microbus 'Rosen aus Steinfurth'.

T2a Panelvan 'Esso' (EM).

T2b Pick-Up with enlarged bed 'Philipp Holzmann'.

LEFT: T2a Panelvan 'Hanseaten Kaffee' (E).
ABOVE: In a dealer's showroom (E).

T2b Microbus with skis on the back.

Side view (top) and back view (bottom) of the Kemperink converion 'Bahlsen' (B).

T2b Kombi 'Kärcher' with trailer (AK).

ABOVE AND ABOVE RIGHT: *T2a Money Transporter 'Geld + Wert Transporte Fritz Kötter' (WT).*

BELOW: *T2b Money Transporter 'Ziemann' (WT).*

TOP: *T2a/b Pick-Up oil transporter.*

ABOVE: *T2a/b Pick-Up oil transporter, tank equipment.*

LEFT: *T2a/b Pick-Up of 'Nederlandse Wegenmarkering', a Dutch road marker.*

ABOVE LEFT: T2b Kombi 'DHL' (KM).   *ABOVE*: T2a Kombi service Bus 'BDF' (RR).

LEFT: T2b Electric Panelvan 'Flughafen Frankfurt' (MS).

T2b Kombi High-Roof 'Ice-Bus' conversion.   Curious conversion: T2b Kombi as a tower on a gliding field.

Ferdinand Mühlens

TOP: T2b Panelvan '4711' coloured in SK 9541(R).

LEFT: T2b Panelvan '4711', back (R).

ABOVE: T2a Panelvan 'Patrizier Lavende' (R).

Seba Dynatronic

In the 1970s the German company Seba Dynatronic – specializing in cable testing, diagnosis and fault detection – was operating with a huge fleet of T2 measuring vehicles. These Bay Windows were usually painted in orange and white (SK 9225).

TOP ROW: *Front views of the T2b Kombi 'Seba Dynatronic' (SD).*
BOTTOM ROW: *Rear views of the T2b Kombi 'Seba Dynatronic' (SD).*

ABOVE LEFT: *T2b Panelvan 'Miele' – SK 9314 Miele Red (M).*
LEFT: *T2a Kombi measuring vehicle with compressor trailer (SD).*
ABOVE: *Measuring instruments inside the Bus (SD).*

Present for the Peoples Republic of China consigned during a state visit of the German Chancellor Helmut Schmidt in 1976.

Otto Versand

MAIN PIC: *Fleet of T2b Panelvans 'Otto'.* INSET: *T2b Panelvan 'OTTO Kundendienst'.*
BOTH PICTURES COPYRIGHT *OTTO-PRESSEBILD.*

ABOVE: T2b Pick-Up with enlarged bed 'Kabelmetal'.

RIGHT: T2a Kombi High-Roof 'Kabelmetal'.

JACOBS KAFFEE FLEET

In the 1950s, the Jacobs Kaffee company, located in Bremen (Germany), installed the VW Transporter as a delivery van. The Jacobs Buses had two different exterior trims. Deliveries to retailers were made in black and yellow Transporters, nicknamed 'bumble-bees' because of their body paint. The wholesale trade was serviced by white- and brown-coloured Bay Windows with the lettering 'Multiplan'. The slogan 'Wonderful Jacobs Coffee' was adapted for each country of distribution.

All Jacobs Transporters had certain additional equipment as standard, for example, a shelf fitted in the cargo compartment. Jacobs used VW Transporters for delivery up to the beginning of the 1980s; the last ones in use were T3 Panelvans.

The very rare T2b (see box below), built on chassis number 219 2 093 183, is the only known Panelvan in existence today, of over 400 Transporters (Type II, T1–T3) used by Jacobs Kaffee. Manufactured on 12 February 1979, this T2b Bay Window left the factory three days later. It has the modified Type I 1600cc engine with 50bhp.

In model year 1979 the group codes GN1, H61 and K38 represent the following collection of M-codes:

- GN1 = M032, M127, M221, M510;

Presentation of a special Bus

The Jacobs delivery Bus shown here was the first to achieve 100,000km with its original engine. Usually, these engines, under similar heavy use, would last only up to around 50,000km. In this case, the Jacobs employee on the right got a brand-new T2b Panelvan.

- H61 = M171, M184;
- K38 = M145, M181, M500.

The entire Jacobs fleet was painted in a special colour, numbered on the M-plate

9005 (= SK 9005), and only available for Jacobs. SK means *Sonderlackierung* (special painting instructions). The process department at the Hannover factory had specific instructions on how

LEFT: Austrian version of the Jacobs Panelvan (K).
BELOW LEFT: French version of the Jacobs Panelvan (K).
BELOW: Front of the Austrian version (K).

to paint each body part of a Bus. The instructions for Jacobs Transporters were as follows:

- body – roof = Yellow (L263);
- body – upper part with front = Yellow (L263);
- body – lower part without front = Ebony Black (L041);
- cover outer body side quarter panel = Yellow (L263);
- cabin, inside = Yellow (L263);
- cargo compartment, inside and lid engine sealing = Light Beige;
- engine lid = Ebony Black (L041);
- rear panel, inside = Yellow (L263);
- rim = Yellow (L263).

All the Jacobs Panelvans had wooden shelves inside the cargo compartment. The compartment in the back over the engine was partitioned off from the

Fleet of Jacobs Kaffee T2a Panelvans (K).

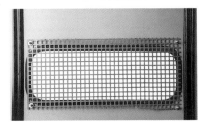

cargo compartment by a board. Another special feature was a grille on the window, in the upper division between cabin and cargo compartment. The extra features of these vehicles were added to the Buses after they left the factory in Hannover. The rear of the Buses had

M-plate of the Jacobs Kaffee Panelvan

92 093 183
100 162 215 663 761
9005NP GN1 H61 K38 065
07 2 7011 121 2110 11

no advertising at all. For special advertising campaigns, a banner was fixed to the outside of the rear panel.

ZDF

Founded in 1963, the ZDF (Zweites Deutsches Fernsehen) is Germany's second television channel. Its employees used the VW Transporter daily as a small and flexible broadcasting vehicle (*see* right). The Panelvan 'R3' was fitted out with two sliding doors and an air-conditioning unit positioned in the front on top of the roof. As an extra option, the T2b Kombi 'R4' received sliding windows fitted into the sliding door and on the opposite side.

The Vaillant Fleet

Established in 1894, Vaillant is a big German company producing gas, electric and oil heating. Like Jacobs Kaffee, Vaillant used Panelvans all over Europe for customer-service purposes.

T2b Panelvan broadcasting vehicle R3 'ZDF' (ZDF/Peter Göbbels).

T2b Kombi broadcasting vehicle R4 'ZDF' (ZDF/Peter Göbbels).

Brazilian transporters at work

all pictures AG

KLAUS ESSER PANELVAN

The Panelvan shown here is owned by Alexander Prinz. It was built on 21 January 1970 with chassis number 210 120 055 and left the Hannover factory on 23 January. All the necessary data of this Bus are shown on the M-plate. In model year 1970 the group code C77 represents the M-codes M500 and M510. This T2a has the typical Type I 1600cc engine with 47bhp.

The first registration of this Panelvan was on 28 April 1970, with the German number GV-AJ 249. Its first owner was the company Klaus Esser KG, located in Norf, close to Düsseldorf. This company – producing light domes, roof draining and fire alarm systems – had a huge fleet of passenger cars, trucks, coaches and light commercial vehicles with about thirty Bay Window Buses. Panelvans were used as service vehicles, while Microbuses served for staff transportation purposes. The employee living furthest away from the Esser factory was entrusted with a Microbus, and expected to pick up his colleagues on his way to work. During the day the Buses were used for running errands, delivering mail, or collecting visitors at the airport or railway station. At the same time, the vehicles also served a purpose in publicizing the company and helping to improve its branding. Indeed, its effective and unusual body design won Klaus Esser KG the first German marketing prize, in 1973.

For Klaus Esser, managing director of the company, care of the vehicles was of the utmost importance. None of his employees was ever allowed to leave the factory with an unclean vehicle.

The Panelvan shown here was used from 1970 to 1972 as a service vehicle, for installing light domes. In 1972 it was handed over, probably as a gift, to the fire brigade in Neuss. It was given a red and white fire brigade paint job and a blue rotating light with sirens. It was used for transportation purposes until 1996. After that, it had two private owners, the second of whom did some restoration work on it, and gave it back its original colour of Light Grey. After buying the Bus in 2001, the present owner completely stripped down the vehicle and restored it. With the help of Rainer Esser – son of the former managing director – the striking original paint combination and lettering have been reproduced.

T2a Panelvan 'Klaus Esser KG'.

Back of the Klaus Esser Panelvan.

M-Plate of the Esser Panelvan

```
02  120  055

414151  C77  065  507
04 4  7084  070  2110  11
```

Company logo.

Photograph of the Esser fleet in the early 1970s.

glossary

Bay Window Nickname for the second generation of the Transporters (1967–79). 'Bay Window' comes from the 'bay view' you have through the windshield in comparison to its predecessor.

Breadloaf Nickname for second generation of the Transporters (1967–79). Given to the Car because it is shaped somewhat like a loaf of bread.

CKD Completely Knocked Down. Vehicle was shipped in parts to a factory outside Germany where it was assembled and sold. This method was used to avoid high import taxes on cars.

Clipper The name given by Volkswagen to the Microbus. The Microbus Deluxe was called 'Clipper L'. The word 'Clipper' was used only in the August 1967 brochure because Pan Am had already registered the name. Many enthusiasts still use the name to designate an early Bay Window Microbus.

Chassis plate Plate with the chassis number (also known as VIN) and the maximum axle loads.

Combi This word is used instead of 'Kombi' in some countries.

Crew Cab Pick-up model with an enlarged cabin so a 'crew' of up to 6 people can sit in it.

DIN 'Deutsche Industrie Norm', a German industry standard.

Kombi Delivery van with windows in cargo compartment. Also available with seats in cargo compartment. In Australia, 'Kombi' is the general word for all Volkswagen buses.

Loaf See 'Breadloaf'.

LHD Left Hand Drive.

Model Year A model year always starts in the August before the actual calender year begins, and runs until the July of the calender year. For example, the model year 1970 ran from August 1969 until July 1970.

M-code Optional extra or lesser equipment on a Transporter. The 'M' comes from the German term 'Mehr-und Min-derausstattung'.

M-plate Plate with production details, fixed in every German-assembled Transporter.

M-specification Variations to the standard model that is mentioned under an M-code.

Panelvan Delivery van with no windows in the side panels of the cargo compartment.

RHD Right Hand Drive.

SK *Sonderlackierung*; special painting instructions.

T1 Denotes a first generation Transporter (i.e. 1950–67), also known as 'Split Screen vans'.

T2, T2a, T2b 'T2' stands for 'Transporter 2nd generation' (i.e. 1967–79). T2a is the name for the early type (1968–71), while T2a/b is the name for the 1972 model year that looks partially like a T2a but also shows signs of the T2b. T2b is the name for the later types (1973–79).

Transporter The name under which the Type 2 was sold in English-speaking countries in the period 1950–79. In most countries VW simply presented it as 'the VW company car' or 'VW Bus'. The model that replaced the Bay Window in 1979 got the name 'Transporter' officially all over the world.

Type 1 engine The name for the type of air-cooled boxer engine that was applied for the first time in the Beetle ('VW' Type 1'). The Type 1 engine was built in 1200, 1300, 1500 and 1600cc variations. Of these only the 1300 and 1600cc engines were used in the Bay Window. For an explanation of types, *see also* 'Type 2'.

Type 2 The Volkswagen Transporter. The first type of car built by Volkswagen was the Beetle. In technical articles the Beetle and all cars derived from it were called 'Type 1'. The Transporter was the second type of car they took into production: hence all Transporter-derived vehicles are called 'Type 2'.

Type 4 engine The name for the type of air-cooled boxer engine that was used for the first time in the VW 411 ('VW Type 4'). The type 4 engine was built in 1700, 1800 and 2000cc variations. All of these were used in the Bay Window. For an explanation of types, *see also* 'Type 2'.

VIN Vehicle Identification Number, also known as 'chassis number'.

VWoA Volkswagen of America.

Zwitter German name for the 1972 model, which is the link between the early (T2a) and later (T2b) types of the Bay Window.

index